RADICAL RETIREMENT ROADMAP

Creating Your Ideal Retirement
STARTING TODAY!

R. J. KELLY

AEP, CAP, ChFC, CLU, MSFS, RICP, WMCP

with CAITLIN TAYLOR

R. J. Kelly-- 1st ed.
ISBN: 978-1-954757-70-7

To my mother, Kathryn "Kay" Kelly, who embodied kindness, grace, and quiet courage. Born to a humble wheat-and-cattle family in northeast Montana. She was blind in one eye, but never let that stop her from reading aloud to children at our community center, often with two or three nestled on her lap. A soprano soloist, a woman of deep faith, and my biggest fan! I could do no wrong in her eyes. I strive every day to live up to the version of me she believed in. I look forward to seeing her again in Heaven!

Contents

Section 4: How Many?

Section 5: How Come?

Section 6: How to Start?

Introduction

Currently, from what I see, most Americans are in trouble! Not just politically, morally, relationally, physically, but fiscally! But before I give you all the numbers, let me tell you how I got here.

Many years ago, I completed the Retirement Income Certified Professional (RICP) designation credentialing program. It is a wonderful professional education curriculum offered by the American College in Bryn Mawr, PA. (Shout out to the folks there—they have a bunch of great professional education programs available!)

As I read about the degree to which Americans are unprepared for retirement, I was both shocked and worried—so concerned, in fact, that I decided to create a "short" video on the topic.

That "short" video became a twelve-video series, which has now become the general foundation for this book and a course on creating a radical retirement! (Side note: Be very careful of those "short" projects and passion topics … you may find yourself creating a three-minute video only to find that it leads to a book, online classes, TED talks, and more!)

As another aside, after further research, I have realized that retirement "unpreparedness" (is that a word?) is not an issue exclusive to Americans, but appears to be a global issue.

For the curious, you can find that video series on our YouTube channel "Wealth Legacy Group" under "Top 10 Retirement Planning Mistakes." (But do that later!)

According to a Bankrate December 2023 Survey of Americans:

- Only 44% have enough money in savings to cover an unexpected $1,000 expense
- The remaining 56% would need to fund their emergency by:
    - Using a credit card
    - Spending less in other areas
    - Borrowing from friends/family
    - Taking out a personal loan

Given the above lack of funds for an emergency, retirement "unpreparedness" is a major epidemic for which we don't (unfortunately) have a vaccine available.

Successful retirement doesn't happen automatically. We must be intentional in our planning, which is why most Americans, Canadians, fill in the nationality ______, don't retire well. We spend more time planning for vacations than we do for our 20-40 year retirement.

The Northwestern Mutual 2023 Planning & Progress Study reports that:

- 21% of Americans have nothing saved for retirement (Holy cow!)
- 31% have saved less than $5,000
- 11% aren't even sure what they have! (Scary thought! If this is you, go pull your investment statements *right now*, then come back!)
- 33% of Boomers have less than $25,000 in retirement savings
- 78% of Americans say they are "extremely" or "somewhat worried" about running out of money in retirement (They should be!)
- Over 50% expect to work past age 65 "out of necessity" – not because they love working

Northwestern Mutual's 2025 Planning & Progress study is not comforting either:

- 46% of people not-yet-retired think they will NOT be financially prepared for retirement
- 51% of Americans think it's somewhat or very likely that they will outlive their savings
- Only 27% of Boomers (26% of Gen X) are planning on delaying their Social Security benefits to maximize the amount they receive
- But the good news is that Gen Z and Millennials are paying attention! They started saving for retirement (on average) at ages 24 and 29, respectively. Compare

that to Gen X's average starting age of 33 and Boomers beginning at 37

With all this background, this book is a result of my 35+ years of helping clients as a Retirement Income Certified Professional, independent fee-based Registered Investment Advisor, and Chartered Financial Consultant (and a few other professional designations).

The sole purpose of this book is to help you build an *amazing* roadmap for a spectacular retirement—no matter when you start!

Just to let you know, we will be exploding some long-time truisms that frankly just "ain't" true anymore. (Sorry for the grammar, Mr. Paulsen.)

For example, common "rules" like:

- ***"Save 10x your income by a certain age."***
  - Wait … that doesn't consider lifestyle or desires
  - It also doesn't consider others that you may be caring for … your retirement "world" is often bigger than just you!
  - Good news … we'll tell you in a later chapter how you can make up for lost time!

We are more than one-dimensional. In addition to the financial needs, how do we address the relational, emotional, spiritual, mental, and physical needs of retirement?

P.S. My compliance attorney advised me to include the obligatory disclaimer when discussing investing and returns: ***Past performance is not a guarantee of future results.*** *Investing involves risk, and it's possible to lose everything.* Although if you understand your investments, get good counsel (professional advice, not your uncle with the hair-brained schemes), and don't risk more than you can afford to lose, then anything is possible!

P.P.S. My co-writer and I would like to make a quick note on generational writing styles. Boomers tend to use "quotes" for emphasis (italics/bold were not an option on typewriters!) … and ellipses to indicate a pause. Language changes. To Millennials and younger generations, these grammatical tools have often come to mean "sarcasm" and … passive-aggressive subtext. We worked on this book out of a desire to give people tools and hope for a better future. Please read the quotes as a "technical (-ish) term" … and ellipses a pause for breath.

CHAPTER SUMMARY

The Five How Questions

Building a map of and toward your retirement provides you with critical mileposts, so you aren't throwing darts blindfolded and hoping that one of them hits.

Major takeaways from this chapter will include:

- How to specifically define what retirement looks like to you
- Where does age 65 come from as retirement age, and is that the "right" age for you?
- The five questions you must answer to create your "ideal retirement plan"

The Five How Questions

How would you feel about driving on a road without any lines? No signs? Nothing to tell you if you're headed toward your destination or even in the right lane? Somehow, I think you would either slow down or try to find an exit, so that you could get your bearings and figure out where you are. Can you even call AAA this far out of town? I would certainly lock my doors if they weren't locked already!

That's exactly what I find with new clients and friends the first time we talk about retirement. They don't know where the road leads or even where they should stop for gas or snacks along the way.

For example, to make this very personal, can you answer the Five How Questions for yourself?

Can you tell me specifically:

- **How soon?**
    - That is, what *exact* age do you plan on retiring?

- **How much?**
    - How much will you need at that point? Before or after tax?
    - Will that include a provision for some sort of adjustment over time … a "cost-of-living" increase?

- **How long?**
    - How long do you expect to live?
    - Spoiler alert: according to the latest research, it's a LOT longer than most people imagine! (We'll be discussing life expectancy in a later chapter.)

- **How many?**
    - How many different sources of income will you have to draw from?
    - Will at least one source provide non-taxable income?

Perhaps the most important "How" question of them all …

- **How come?**
    - Why do you want to retire?
    - What are your reasons for wanting to "retire?" (Retiring "from" without a retiring "to" is a frequent cause of premature death … more on this later.)
    - What legacy of positive impact will you create?
    - How will the world be a better place because *you* are here?

I call these the "Five Hows" for obvious reasons! And it's here where I believe things need to start. It's long before the "rates of return" discussion - as important as that is - or really before anything else.

Stephen Covey, in his blockbuster book *The 7 Habits of Highly Effective People*, taught us to "Begin with the end in mind."

This is just as true with retirement planning as it is for anything else important in our lives. Most people simply have NOT envisioned what they want for their retirement. With clarity comes action. No clarity … no actions.

Surprisingly, asking specific questions about what retirement looks like often draws a vacant stare. Many people have not taken the time to clarify what retirement means to them, beyond the thought of spending additional time with loved ones, playing more rounds of golf (or taking lessons!), and tackling their "bucket list" (if they even have one).

How about you? What does retirement look like to you?

And what would you say are at least three compelling reasons why you want to retire someday?

Oh … and while we're at it … when?

More have an immediate answer as to the "when" question because it has been drilled into our psyche for most of us since birth. Everyone all together now … "AGE 65!"

Again, why? Why age 65? (OK… some are saying age 66 or age 67 because your full Social Security benefits kick in then, but you get the point. Right?)

For most of us, we have been told age 65 so often that we assume it has certain mysterious properties, as if it were a relic of time. Or is it a rite of passage akin to getting our driver's license or legally having our first drink of an adult beverage? In a way, it is.

Where do we first see age 65 being set as the "official age" for retirement? Inquiring minds want to know!

How Did Government-Sponsored Retirement Come About?

The first state-sponsored retirement system originated in Germany in 1889, proposed by Chancellor Otto von Bismarck. He initially proposed the age of 70, but the German government eventually reduced the age to 65 roughly a decade later. (Nothing said about beer rations, by the way. I think that comes automatically in Germany, regardless of retirement age!)

Back then, age 65 was the equivalent of age 110 today! No wonder they chose that age. Very, very few ever got there!

With that precedent, when America established the Social Security program in 1935, we likewise chose age 65. There was no actuarial planning that went into either the selection of age or benefits.

(Actuaries, by the way, are very smart math folks who figure out statistics and how to apply them to the real world for governments, banks, insurance companies, etc.)

In 1930, life expectancy for men was 58, and for women, it was 62. So again, age 65 was an age few were expected to reach. It was never intended to be a "pay you 'til you drop" kind of thing. It has become that, however … again, without any kind of prudent actuarial planning.

Because of enhanced life expectancies, it is now expected that Social Security benefits will be reduced to 77% in 2034 unless Congress pulls a rabbit out of the hat! Additionally, the healthcare system, Medicare, is projected to reach a point of negative funding, where more is paid out than received, by the year 2029.

We'll get into this more later in the book, but in America ... just because ... half of the population begins their Social Security income at age 62! People take this despite having, in most cases, a 30% "haircut" on their benefits rather than waiting until the "normal retirement age" of 65, 66, or 67 (again, depending on your age).

Here's a radical thought ... rather than retiring at the first opportunity or because "it's just what you do,"... how about spending some time first considering the "why?" before the "how soon?" Coming up with solid reasons for your "why?" will not only give you a better pinpoint on the optimal retirement age for you, but might also give you more years to spend in retirement happily!

What Makes People Happy? Less Anxious?

In Daniel Pink's book *Drive*, he discusses a study conducted by the University of Rochester every year with its graduating class. The research team surveys graduating students about their future aspirations. Then, they sort the aspirations into "extrinsic" goals, such as becoming wealthy, and "intrinsic" goals, such as continued learning or helping others.

The researchers found, upon following up with the students years later in their careers, that the newly minted adults with intrinsic goals (also called "purpose" goals) had "higher levels of satisfaction and subjective well-being than when they were in college, and quite low levels of anxiety and depression."

But what about the graduates motivated by wealth or fame?

Their self-esteem and satisfaction with their lives were about the same as when they were students. They also showed higher rates of anxiety and depression.

What Are You Retiring *To*?

Now that you're thinking about how soon (or maybe rethinking), what about how you want to live? Do you want to travel the world? Start up a passion business? Get involved in volunteering? What about enjoying time with the grandchildren?

Because some of those activities will require more monthly income than others.

I've found that the easiest way to start thinking of it is to ask yourself: *Will what I want to do with my retired years cost more, less, or about the same as what I spend now?*

If you're looking forward to spending your time catching up on all that reading you meant to do, volunteering, and not doing so much travel, then you'll likely need about 75% of your current income in retirement.

If you're planning on keeping life just about the same as it is now, that works out to about 85% of your current income.

But, if you're one of the people who are going to leap onto the nearest ship/jet/RV and see the world, you'll need roughly

105% of your current annual income to make the books work for your ideal retirement!

There are many ways to slice the pie in categorizing retirement. A fascinating look at many facets of retirement for Boomers is Ken Dychtwald's *What Retirees Want.* He categorizes retirees into categories based on their preparedness and attitudes toward retirement. The descriptions below are quoted from him because he does a great job of making each category crystal clear.

Ageless Explorers (~20%) "...see retirement as a time of opportunity, adventure, exploration, and personal reinvention…They are financially secure in retirement through the recombination of successful careers, financial knowledge and planning, and the fact of saving for 25 years (the most of any segment)... [They] have rejected the life-of-leisure definition of retirement in favor of exercising their freedom to choose new paths."

Comfortably Contents (~20%) "...approach retirement with a more traditional, less driven view that retirement is a reward for a life of conscientious work…their focus is on recreation, fun, and relaxation…They are the most likely of the four segments to say they are having fun and are very happy and healthy in retirement."

Live for Todays (~20%) "have had active and varied lives and hope to continue with new experiences and adventures in retirement...They have the biggest list of things they'd like to do and would ideally like their retirement to be an extension of their free-spirited lives... They're not planners...They may have done OK financially, but it was more a matter of pay-as-you-go than save-for-retirement... Because most haven't planned or saved enough to live comfortably in retirement, they are frustrated with the financial challenges they face in this stage of life."

Worried Strugglers (~35%) "are, compared with the other segments, the least ready and able to enjoy retirement. They have fewer financial resources and fewer hopes and dreams for what they'd like to do. They report being more worried, less active, less healthy, and less happy...For this segment, retirement is not the 'golden years,' but instead a largely unpleasant experience. Yet they report that they're not giving up and most think of themselves as pragmatic, as survivors."

In my friend Clay Gilespie's wonderful book on retirement, *Create the Retirement You Really Want*, he uses the same categories but has more specific numbers, which we used above. He's also in Canada, which likely has slightly different demographics than the good old US of A.

So...what does that all tell us? I know which category I'd like to fall into and can guess that if you're reading this book, you're likely aiming for either Ageless Explorer or Comfortably Content, too.

By the way, the good news is that, on average, the Ageless Explorers have only been saving for retirement for 25 years. It's not something you have to start when you are 20 years old - although I certainly wouldn't try to talk you out of getting started that young!

Picking one of the above categories helps create an idea of what you are retiring to or whether you want to retire at all. Maybe instead of enjoying a rest well earned, you'll start a business just for fun or write that novel that has been sitting in the file cabinet for 17 years.

I have a friend who didn't plan out his "retiring to" very well. OK, he didn't plan it at all. He had a demanding, high-stress legal career and was ready to kick back and live the good life.

The good life didn't last very long. After several months, he'd seen *every* movie that was in theaters. He is a very social guy, so staying in the house all day was not good for him. Turns out, even though he had been looking forward to relaxing for years, he got downright bored…another type of stress altogether.

After some soul-searching, he ended up starting a consulting business to keep himself occupied and found ways to volunteer his expertise in his community for people who otherwise couldn't afford it.

He found his path. But had he considered what he would be retiring *to* rather than *from*, he would have saved himself a couple of years of frustration.

And what you're retiring to may change. There are some often-cited changes called the Four Phases of Retirement. And it's something to keep in mind as you plan what you want to do. To paraphrase:

The Go-Go Phase - You're so happy to be retired! You have all of this time! You're making all of those folks giving motivational speeches look bad with your energy and enthusiasm.

The Slow-Go Phase - You may have overdone it in the previous phase. Now, you will likely pull back and seek more balance between your adventures and enjoying time in your home or nearby communities.

The Why-Go Phase - You've done all you wanted to do. Why do it again? If you've been on ten different cruises and it's not your all-consuming passion, why keep doing it?

The No-Go Phase - This is where health typically starts to decline. Travel becomes difficult, and more money is being spent on healthcare costs rather than on adventures. It doesn't necessarily bring a decrease in spending. The spending simply changes.

Your Money's Life Expectancy

Our third question is, "How long will you need this income?" or "How long do you expect to live?"

It's a tricky question because it's a lot longer than most people think. Did you know that if you reach age 60 today, you have over 50% chance of living another 20-25 years (depending on whether you're male or female)?

That's a good decade more than the national average life expectancy. According to the Wall Street Journal, there is an 18% chance that at least one spouse in a couple will live to age 95.

Just for fun, you can see your own life expectancy estimates from the Social Security Administration by entering your birthday at https://www.ssa.gov/oact/population/longevity.html.

But is it wise to plan to live an average life expectancy? Even if you've decided to join me in living to age 147 (hey, I want to celebrate the year 2100), what type of investments do you need to make sure your money lasts that long?

There are investment platforms available that provide built-in stop-loss mechanisms to ensure you don't need to spend years recovering from a market downturn, which can keep your portfolio afloat after you're no longer actively contributing to it. There are other investment vehicles, such as certain types of annuities. We'll dive into how to set up your portfolio to (most likely) outlive you in Section 3. Just some food for thought right now because you will likely live longer than your parents or grandparents. Just sayin'!

Where Does All This Money Come From?

Which leads us to the next question of … "How many?" By that, I mean, how many buckets of income will you have to draw from? And not just how many buckets will you need or want for income, but how many buckets will you fill for your spouse, your kids, grandkids, community, or charity?

I promise we will go into all sorts of detail on these buckets in Section 4. But here's the idea in the meantime.

Each bucket of income has different tax treatments and behaves differently in economic cycles (most of the time). You might be familiar with a 401(k). That's one bucket. Retirees and soon-to-be-retirees are commonly offered annuities as a way to "never outlive your money." That's another bucket, and we'll talk about both annuities and how to avoid outliving your money. Your emergency savings is a bucket. Rental real estate could be another bucket. You get the idea by now.

The Point of It All

Finally, the last of the Five How Questions asks, "How come?"

What are the reasons you want to retire? Or, what are the reasons that somebody told you that you're supposed to, and, like many Americans, are doing it blindly without asking why?

What are the reasons you personally want to retire? Maybe you don't have a good answer to that.

In which case, GOOD!

Retirement is, for the most part, really not good for your health. One of the quickest ways to die is to retire *from* something without retiring *to* something. And guess what happens? You won't want to buy green bananas!

But let's challenge one another to find reasons that aren't just about you or me. Let's make it bigger than that.

We've helped clients who worked incredibly hard to break into the "Three Comma Club" (they amassed over $1 billion). One, in particular, comes to mind, and I will call him James. I met James when he recently divorced his fourth wife. His health was declining, and we started on some estate planning. He had gobs of money and didn't have much of a social network. His children and grandchildren avoided him at best. He didn't care much for them, either.

Mark Twain, the legendary humorist, once said, "The two most important days in your life are the day you are born and the day you find out why."

Our client, James, never did figure out the "why," although he was certainly very financially successful.

We also worked with another woman, whom we'll call Irene. She was a school secretary who had been forced out of her job because of arthritis. She took what little savings she had and bought a house, fixed it up, and rented it out. Then, she repeated this process ten more times until she had a tidy income each month. And, perhaps as important from a long-term planning perspective, she was building equity in these houses.

I don't recall where she got this idea or strategy, as she came to us as she was getting older and wanted to ensure that her estate plan aligned with her values. We set it up so that upon her death, her two children would get two houses each. With the idea that they'd have one to live in if they wanted, and one to rent. The other six homes would be donated to her charities and her church. (Setting this up ahead of time and making sure she wouldn't change her mind also let us get her some fantastic tax deductions.)

Irene, unlike James, knew what she valued in life – family and community. She modeled her finances the way she modeled her life, giving her excess time, energy, and money to folks who needed it.

Keep your long-term purpose in mind as you plan for retirement. I believe everyone has one. We just have to discover it … or create it!

Assuming you haven't gone out for ice cream or called the work colleague who still owes you $50, you have made it to the end of this chapter! Congratulations! Hopefully, you have started to think (or think more) about answers to your Five How Questions:

- How much are you going to need or want for income?
- How soon will you need/want to retire?

- How long should you project needing that income?
- How many buckets of income will you have, and how many people will you need to provide for?
- How will your life have a positive impact on our world?

What's next?

How about a few questions to get your specific answers? Let's dig into the Five How Questions for your own situation. For you perfectionists out there (I "are" one, by the way!) … don't get hung up on having the "right answers." If you don't have an age in mind (I didn't for the longest time), just plug something in. You can fine-tune it later as you continue to gain more clarity in the weeks, months, or years ahead.

Check out the questions we have for you at the end of this chapter. These are critically important answers to help you get clear on whether you will have the amazing retirement you deserve.

Action Items

Your "homework" for this chapter is to find several clean sheets of paper (or more!) and start sketching out your very own answers to the Five How Questions. Don't worry. You should not expect "perfect" answers right out of the gate. No. Your answers will likely change along the way. It happens to us all at this early stage. We're just getting started!

Ask yourself:

1. **How soon do I want to retire?**
    a. Exactly when do I want to retire? Month and year? What age will I be then?
    b. What is my contingency plan if I am forced to retire early due to work, health, or family reasons?
2. **At a high level, how much income will I need each month?**
    a. And remember, I will still need to pay taxes in retirement - how much will that be?
    b. Will I have any "big ticket" expenses in addition to my monthly spending?
3. **How long?**
    a. What is my projected lifespan? What if I live to be 100 or older?
    b. Complete the https://www.ssa.gov/oact/population/longevity.html Life Expectancy Calculator
4. **How many?**
    a. How many sources of retirement income will I have?
        i. Will any of them be non-taxable?
    b. How many people will my income need to support?
5. **How come?**
    a. Perhaps the most important question to ask myself is, how come? That is *why* do I want to retire, ever, let alone at my chosen age?

    i. What does my ideal retirement look like?
    ii. Do I want to retire at all, or simply change what I'm doing?

b. Do I have a personal (or family) mission statement? If not, this is the time in life to draft one.

CHAPTER SUMMARY

Taking Inventory – The Map, Compass, and a Pyramid

Now that you know what you want your retirement to look like, how do you know where to start? A map doesn't do you any good if you don't know where you are.

Major takeaways from this chapter will include:

- How to take inventory of your starting point
- What is the financial pyramid, and why does it matter?
- How to build each layer of the pyramid and why the order is important
- Note: I've never met anyone in serious financial trouble if they had first built solidly in layers 1 - 3 of the pyramid

Taking Inventory - The Map, Compass, and a Pyramid

Now that you've hopefully arrived at some initial answers to your Five How Questions, you have a compass to start your journey … so let's get started on unfolding the map! (That would be the rest of the book!)

So … what's next?

Have you ever gone to a city that you've never been to before and felt disoriented, or maybe even "honey, please turn down the radio" lost? Like … "Why are there so many poorly marked freeways?" "Which direction is Sequoia Ave, or was it Sequoia Lane?" And "How close is the nearest Starbucks?" (Hey, I'm originally from Washington State. Forgive me, Caribou, Dutch Bros, Coffee Culture, Dunkin Donuts, etc.)

What's next is that you will likely get out your phone and open Google Maps or simply grab a paper map (what's that???) from the front desk and figure out where you are, where you want to go, and the fastest way to get there. Right?

Let's take inventory of where we are and where we want to go. Hold on to your compass (the Five How Questions). Between that and the map, that's going to get you to where you want to go, especially when the storms come in, and you're hungry, lost, and lonely. You can still take out your compass and pinpoint where you need to go.

When others come to me for retirement advice, I'm often asked the following types of questions:

- Should I save before I invest? If so, how much?
- Should I pay down debt before I put money into a 401(k) (or IRA)?
- Where can I get the best returns?
- Is my home an investment?

Surprisingly, very few ask the "crocodile on the couch" question: "*How much should I be saving for retirement? What percentage of my income should I be setting aside now?*"

If I can mix my metaphors, the easiest answer could be described using what we'll call the "financial pyramid," which is something I learned from another financial advisor years ago. (I think the Earth's crust was cooling at the time.) As he described it, like every construction project since the Egyptians, we start with the foundation before adding the layers on top.

This is the 30,000-foot view of the financial pyramid. Most of what we'll be discussing is retirement, also known as the fourth tier. Let's cover what the supporting structures will be for building up the retirement of your dreams.

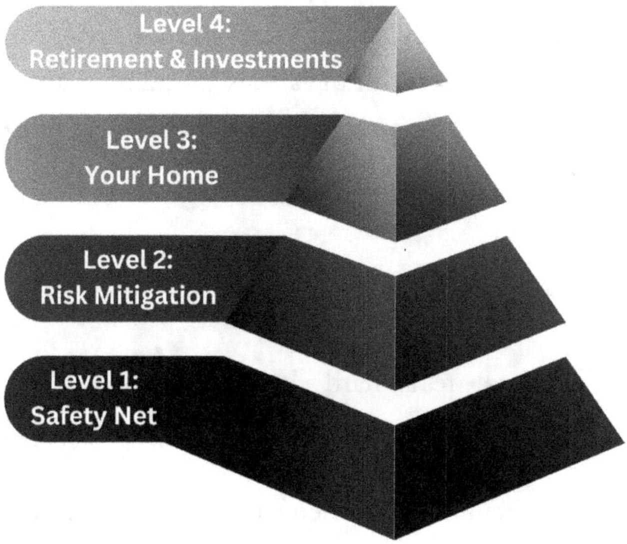

Level 1 - Build Your Safety Net

You have two buckets to fill here, as every other current and future financial decision you make will rest on them. This is your emergency/opportunity fund. It's the quick cash to cover emergencies that inevitably happen. But it also lets you take advantage of opportunities that come your way.

In the first bucket, you ideally have 3 - 6 months of expenses in cash. If you're an entrepreneur or have rental properties, consider having 12 to 24 months in this bucket. Oh, and do put this money into its own stand-alone account. Let's make it more difficult to spend!

The second bucket involves building up 3 - 6 months of expense reserves in the cash values of permanent insurance contracts. This creates a way to tap into additional reserves that are, again, less likely to be spent except for emergencies or opportunities. (We will cover more on this in various "buckets" chapters later on because it's also a tax-advantaged way to build a retirement income stream!)

Level 2 - Risk Mitigation

You worked hard - really hard - building up your safety net in Level 1. Level 2 prevents life from making you start over.

Level 2 is all about building adequate amounts of insurance for a similar purpose.

- Disability insurance protects your income and all that is connected to that … like your house payment, car, kids' school, and so forth
- Life insurance protects you, your family, and your business, and builds assets
- Long-term care insurance protects your retirement savings, your family, and helps you focus on recovery
- Auto, home, or renters, and umbrella liability insurances to cover your assets and give us lots of goofy TV commercials these days!

Level 3 - Home

People treat their homes as assets nowadays, and for most American homeowners, it is their biggest single financial asset. But try not to think of it as an investment. You can have all the investments in the world, but you'll still need a place to live.

The only caveat regarding the above is that if you live in California, New Jersey, New York, or a similar area, you might have $1 million of net worth tied up in the property value of your parking space. If you plan to move to a more affordable state (with fewer loonies on the loose!), you might be able to make a case for why a portion of your home equity counts as retirement funds.

Level 4 - Retirement Accounts & Other Long-Term Investments

Finally! Here's where we start looking at 401(k)s, IRAs, and other retirement assets.

To clarify, this isn't to say that you should buy a house before you start contributing to your 401(k). It is an order of importance, but it also needs to be tempered with reality … I mean, have you *seen* housing prices in California? Yikes.

If you've properly built the first three levels of the financial pyramid, this is where your wealth can start to grow exponentially.

For example, you can diversify your real estate holdings with rental properties, land, Real Estate Investment Trusts (also called REITs), and perhaps even "private placements" or "Delaware Statutory Trusts." (This assumes you qualify financially as an "accredited investor." More on that later in the chapter "Investment Buckets for Accredited Investors!")

You'll get into more in-depth investing in equities (stocks, bonds, mutual funds, exchange-traded funds, and so forth) or even explore crypto at this level of the pyramid. (Getting a tattoo is optional for this class of investment.)

This pyramid has worked for me, multiple clients, and any of my friends and family who will listen. It sounds really boring, and it is. It requires extreme patience because it isn't terribly sexy. This approach doesn't give you stories to tell at a cocktail party of your 1,000% return on a random stamp investment you made at an artificial intelligence convention. Nope, pretty darn boring ... but oh so successful, lower risk, happier spouses, and better nighttime sleep!

In fact, just to really make the point, I haven't met anybody who got into serious financial trouble once they built up the first three tiers of their financial pyramid. But I've met plenty of people in huge financial trouble who violated the discipline of building up their financial pyramid. They invested before they saved and insured ... and didn't have the financial reserves to withstand the unforeseen financial tidal wave that hit them out of the blue. It isn't how much you earn. It is how much you set aside to be prepared that will make the biggest difference for you over the years.

Even if you haven't fully built the stable base of your financial pyramid yet, don't give up. Keep putting money away so that when you are ready to set aside retirement funds, you won't have to pull them out to pay for an unexpected financial crisis.

It might take years to build the first two layers. And that's OK.

You'll find that as you regularly set money aside and watch it accumulate, you create a "positive addiction" to saving, which we'll discuss in a later chapter.

The point is to build an emergency and opportunity fund first. Before you do anything else, join the 44% of Americans who can cover a $1,000 expense. Then get one, then two, then three months of expenses saved up.

Once you have some breathing room, start on the next steps of the pyramid. And, every once in a while, take a moment to appreciate the view and see how far you've come as you climb!

Action Items

1. **Using your notepad or notebook, mark your current position on each level of the financial pyramid. Or use the downloadable sheet from** https://wealthlegacygroup.com/radical-retirement-roadmap-printables
2. **Level 1**
    a. Do you have 3-6 months' worth of expenses saved in a savings account?

   b. Do you have 3-6 months of expenses built up in the cash value of an "investment grade" life insurance contract?

3. **Level 2**
   a. Disability insurance?
   b. Life insurance?
   c. Long-term care insurance?
   d. Home insurance?
   e. Auto insurance?
   f. Umbrella Liability insurance?
4. **Level 3**
   a. Do you own a home or condo? If not, are you saving for a down payment?
5. **Level 4**
   a. Are you maxing out your retirement account contributions?
   b. Do you have a diversified investment portfolio?

SECTION 1

How Much?

CHAPTER SUMMARY

How Much Will You Need In Retirement?

Asking "how much do I need to retire?" is like asking, "what does it cost to travel the world?" It really depends on where you're going and what you want to do when you get there.

In this chapter, you'll learn how to determine "how much will I need?" and then how to set your planning goals ... taking into account what your income is now to build the retirement you wish for.

Major takeaways from this chapter will include:

- Why "How Much?" hinges on what type of lifestyle you want in retirement
- The questions you need to ask yourself about your ideal retirement lifestyle
- Why "How Soon?" factors into "How Much?"
- Questions to answer if you don't plan to retire fully
- Determining if you are a 75%, 85%, or 105% kind of retiree
- The 4% rule

How Much Will You Need In Retirement?

What a great question!

The first of our Five How Questions is one that very few can answer in my experience ... despite how often it comes up in conversations.

Ironically, as we began editing this section of the book, I received an email from a dear friend, whom I will call John. (Not his real name.) "R. J., how much income do you think "Stephanie" and I will need to have when we retire to live the retirement dream we've been picturing?"

My usual response to a question like that asked by my friend is to ask a question in return that helps illustrate the range of answers that might be given.

"John, if I were a travel agent and you asked me how much it would cost for a trip around the world, I would ask you first to describe the details of the trip you have in mind. Where do you want to go? How long do you want to be away? Do you want the "no-star but cultural experience" type of hotel, or first-class trip accommodations? The more specifics you have about your ideal trip, the better I can tell you how much it will cost."

By the way … if you were born after 1990 or so … you may need to Google "travel agent." I do think there are some left out there, but they seem to be few and far between.

"How much" takes some thought … because it is interwoven with how much you will need for the lifestyle you picture … which is interwoven with the remaining four How questions.

Nonetheless, it is a good place to start.

So … for starters … some kick-off questions:

- What major expenses will you have when you retire? Break those up into two categories: one-time vs. ongoing expenses
    - For example, will your home be paid off completely, and will you just need to cover property taxes and insurance? Or will you still be making payments, and if so, for how long?
    - Will you have any debt for the tuition expenses you covered for your kiddos, or help with a down payment on a home, or money for the birth of a grandchild, or grandchildren, or paying for your daughter's wedding?

- Will there be other family members you may be providing for? Parents? Siblings?
- Are there any special non-profits you will continue to support? Either with a one-time donation or ongoing donations?
- Do you have travel plans - and if so, to where and for how long - and at what level of accommodation? (Anyone for that "no-star but cultural experience" I mentioned above? I have a great place to recommend in Kathmandu … but the dogs only sleep during the day and howl all night! Oh, and don't order the chicken! I bent my fork …)
- One-time expenses for a special asset purchase (or two+?)

Once you have begun to outline one-time versus recurring expenses, you can start building your retirement spending plan. For the perfectionists in the group (like me), you won't have it "right" to start with. It is a progressive process that becomes clearer over time. Just beginning the process of putting numbers down is the "perfect" first step and deserves at least an almond croissant!

Next, let's set a "range" to broadly establish the percentage of income to target once you start thinking about the "How soon?" question.

Full disclosure … I never plan to retire fully. For that reason, it has been tough to create my own retirement plan with any specifics. Finally, though, I did target a plan that by a certain age, my home would be completely paid off, and several other rental assets.

Targeting that age when I wanted the debt to be paid off allowed me to work backward and determine how much to pay now.

What I did not anticipate was the surge of adrenaline that came from knowing, absent an unexpected life event, the home and other properties would be free and clear within a specific time frame. Yay! Plus, all that extra income focused on accelerating the mortgage payments would now be available for lifestyle spending! Also, on the rentals, we will have increased income from rising rents. What's not to love about that?

The point is, even if you do not plan to retire fully ever… there are still planning decisions you can make today. Those decisions will dramatically improve your future life (and credit score) by looking ahead to certain freedoms you want by designated points in time.

Forging ahead, here is something else to help further tighten down the "how much?" Do you plan to:

- Keep working the same number of hours you do now (or more?) until they carry you out with your boots on?
- Start your own business or pursue another career or passion that you have been putting off?
- Work less but still generate some income?
- Stop working completely and begin or continue volunteering, or pursue your passions?
- Stop working altogether and become a potted plant?

As you begin answering those questions, it will bring greater clarity on your "income from work" bucket vs. your "income from asset(s)" bucket(s).

One last big-picture choice to consider is: which of the following retirement lifestyle categories best describes the one you are imagining? As well as describing what it looks like, which of the three following descriptions captures your picture of retirement spending?

The first choice is: **"I'll (or we'll) be spending less" because we will ...**

- Have a simpler life
- Likely to be in good health
- Have paid off our home mortgage or paid down significantly, with few other debts
- Have reduced overall expenses
- Do little travel or mostly domestic with little "fluff"

While rare, one of my best friends actually fits the above description of the 75% retirement income. No kids. Rugged backpacker lifestyle. Both he and his wife are very low-maintenance. He is super resourceful and even built their own home. (Yes, there really are people like that still living in America!)

If that captures your vision of retirement, you should be able to get by on roughly 70%—75% of your current income or combined incomes.

But instead, maybe this sounds more like you: **"I'll (or we'll) be spending about the same as now" - a lifestyle very much like today - because we will:**

- Be in good health, but want a cash cushion in case "life happens"
- Spend more time with family and friends
- Have our home paid off or nearly so
- Enjoy traveling from time to time
- Keep busy with hobbies
- Volunteer

If that sounds like you or you and your spouse, you should target roughly 85% of your current income from all sources starting in retirement. Again, this assumes that you will have little to no debt.

This would also be the target range (85% of pre-retirement income) for those who still have a significant debt load and/or owe a large amount on their primary residence.

The last lifestyle category is this: **"I'll (or we'll) be spending more!" because I/we:**

- Will be financially comfortable and likely to have a sizable estate
- May own a vacation home (or two)
- Will be traveling significantly, including overseas travel
- Are not worried about tracking expenses

If this is your vision for retirement, your target should be roughly 105%+ of your current or combined income.

For most Americans, a good target retirement income is 85% of their pre-retirement income.

Now, it's important not to get bogged down in wishful thinking here. I work with a wonderful couple, let's call them Dave and Charlene. When we started their retirement planning years ago, they swore up and down that they were 85% retirees, so that's what we planned for.

They're quickly approaching retirement and now thinking they might want to be 105% people, despite planning for 85%.

We're working on some course corrections to match their "how much?" to their new goals. But the takeaway is that if you are on the fence about what you might want to do in your ideal retirement, choose the higher category! That'll give you some breathing room if you change your mind later.

The next logical question to ask here is, "75%, 85%, or 105% of what?"

Here's how you figure that out…

Take your anticipated last five years of income and average the top three. 75%, 85%, or 105% of that number is a good target retirement income.

Factoring in what your lifestyle will look like after retirement is crucial in planning out your Five Hows.

Then, the question becomes, "How do you get there?"

And, if you want to do some "what–if?" calculations to get you started, there are many different calculators on the web. One that I like, which requires minimal input, is the CalcXML planner. (However, since internet links vanish, you can always do a search for "retirement calculator" to find a free tool.)

So ... whatever amount of income you want each year in retirement, you'll need to accumulate 25x your target annual income as your nest egg ... assuming a 4% withdrawal factor.

What does that mean? Well, to put it in context, with a 4% withdrawal rate for every $100,000, you get $4,000 of income. So, if your target income is $100,000 a year, you would likely want to have $2.5 million accumulated.

In previous decades, you could withdraw 4% of an account indefinitely. Given the lengthened life expectancy and lessened returns, however, we're looking at closer to a 3.5% withdrawal rate without running out of money. This means to withdraw $100,000 a year at 3.5%, you'd need to accumulate $2.86 million instead of $2.5 million.

But in the chapter "Diversifying Income Streams and Sequence of Returns Risk," we'll explore how to withdraw money without running out of it.

Now that you have a placeholder on your financial map, how do you save (and how much should you save) to accumulate the money in the various buckets you will need when you retire?

That's what comes next!

Action Items

1. Determine if you're a 75%, 85%, or 105% retiree.
2. Multiply your current income by 0.75, 0.85, or 1.05 – that's your annual retirement income.
3. Revisit this number every few years. It will change as your income, lifestyle, health, and family situation change.

CHAPTER SUMMARY

How Much Should You Save to Get There?

Great! You have a target nest egg! Now, how do you get from where you are to where you will be before your retirement party? That's what this chapter is all about.

Major takeaways from this chapter will include:

- Revising the old guidelines of 10/10/80 - save 10%, give 10%, and live on 80%
- What is the best advice today for how much you should set aside for retirement?
- Swimming against the stream when it comes to how much to save for future delivery

How Much Should You Save to Get There?

Have you ever heard someone reference a personal financial guideline of saving 10%, giving 10%, and living on the remaining 80%? Ring any bells?

Ah, yes … a simpler time!

I'm having flashbacks of *Back to the Future* … and the old DeLorean, Marty, and the crazy-haired professor. Simple. It seems so long ago, which is when I probably heard the above maxim, 10/10/80.

But how about today????

As for how much to save, I can tell you that the vast majority are not putting away enough to create and live out their ideal retirement! They weren't saving enough, even when the target to defer was 10%, and they certainly aren't today, given the new recommended amounts to set aside.

Let's take a quick poll. Do you believe that we should save:

- Less than 10%?
- The traditional 10%?
- Or would you say, "Are you kidding? Gotta be WAY more!"

Let's check it against the latest numbers … and, yup. If you voted "WAY more," go to the front of the line!

Reason being that we are living much longer than ever before (check out the chapter called "The Longer You Live") … and overall expectations of investment returns are dramatically lower.

Additionally, we are witnessing inflation at rates not seen in over 40 years, which is eroding the net rates of return to negative returns in many cases.

This leads to the point that "just" saving 10% is no longer enough. We need guidelines for our retirement budgeting decisions.

The latest research suggests that we should be saving somewhere between 17% and 18% of our income, not just 10%. All that to say, we should be living on roughly 70% of our income, and paying taxes out of that as well. (Nuts!@#%)

Seventeen percent? Many might say, "That's *crazy!*" Well … no. It's just math. Again, this is because we're living longer, and our overall investment returns are substantially lower. Yikes …

But … don't close this book … yet, at least! There is hope!!

"If I am not even setting aside 5% right now, how am I ever getting to 17%-18%?"

"Sit - stand - walk - run." You get there by making it a goal. And, you can start with small steps and build from there. It's not the *amount* of money you save initially that matters; it's developing a positive addiction to saving money and then increasing the amount being saved over time. (More on this in the next chapter.)

For example, make it a goal to add 1% or 2% each year to your percentage allocation towards retirement. Within 5-10 years, you'll be at that 17% or darned close to it!

Two quick tips.

First, the easiest way to save money is to automate your retirement contributions. Have a set amount going into your retirement accounts. I suggest contributing at least twice a month to an IRA, using smaller amounts more frequently.

Second tip, put your money into things that are not as easy to withdraw from ... somewhere that creates extra "work" or danger (special box on the back of an alligator, anyone?) to get at the money. This could be an account at a different bank or credit union from your primary checking account. Some people put a portion of their money into short-term certificates of deposit. It gets a little bit more money in interest, but it's really about making the money harder to pull out.

As another example, that's the beauty of 401(k)s or other types of retirement accounts. You're adding money, but it's hard to get the cash back out easily.

If you can put up some obstacles to getting your money out, you're probably not going to jump through those hoops unless you absolutely need the cash. But if that money is sitting in a passbook savings account that's linked to your checking account, there's a *really* good chance that you (or someone you love) are going to tap into that money. Been there … done that!

The only goal of your more easily accessible bank account is to accumulate at least three months' worth of living expenses (six is better), as we will discuss next in "Building a Positive Addiction to Saving."

Idealistically, I would love to think that people are donating or giving 10% of their income to others who are less fortunate. (They aren't… hate to spoil the surprise!)

Where I come from, that should be the first step in living a life unshackled by consumerism. It keeps the perspective that there are people in far more difficult financial positions than ourselves.

If you are not a giver, that's OK, but my experience is that those who practice a life of gracious generosity always have more than enough to share. There are charitable organizations that align with nearly every value and will automate donations of $10 per month as a starting point.

Now, if you've kept up with the math, you might be thinking, "But R. J., if I'm supposed to save 17% and give 10%, that leaves me 73% to live on … and pay taxes!"

Great job on keeping up with the mental math!

You might not be there yet. That's OK! Wherever you are in your building of the financial pyramid, keep at it. Living on 73% of your income may involve adjusting your budget, finding ways to increase your income, or a combination of both.

Once you build up to that 17% savings rate, you'll be amazed at how quickly your retirement and savings accounts grow.

So, while I still like watching the movie *Back to the Future*, today the new reality is we need to be putting away far more as a percentage of income (17%) than our parents and grandparents did for future delivery!

Action Items

1. Use your ideal retirement income figure from the last chapter and multiply it by 25 – that assumes a 4% withdrawal rate. (We'll revisit this later.)
2. Calculate a 1% increase from what you're saving now and automate that contribution to saving and/or retirement.

3. Track your spending! Use a spreadsheet, app, or good ol' accounting book.
    a. Do a quick Google search for "best personal expense tracker app" or "how to track monthly expenses" for tactics.

SECTION 2

How Soon?

CHAPTER SUMMARY

Building a Positive Addiction to Saving

Normally, the word "addiction" is not something we associate with good outcomes! However, just as people can get addicted to things that are harmful to themselves and their loved ones, it can also be something used for good! Like what? How about getting "addicted" to putting money away for your own future delivery? Getting positively addicted to saving money! How about that for a mind-bender?

So, the major takeaways from this chapter will include:

- Addiction can be a force for good…or even great!
- How to get "addicted" to saving money
- Where is all of your money going? "Inspect what you expect."
- The benefits of paying cash in a credit card world, and even saving receipts!

Building a Positive Addiction to Saving

For most of us today, when we hear the word "addiction," we think of bad things ... like opioids, gambling, or alcohol addiction. But when was the last time that you thought of the word addiction in a positive way?

Is that even possible?

Well, the reality is that we humans have addictive personalities. (At least most of us do if we're really being honest!) So, suppose you accept the premise that we all have addictive aspects to our personalities. Why not use that tendency for addiction in a positive way?

Like how?

What about getting positively addicted to the idea of saving money? For example, if you want to build an emergency fund (or opportunity fund) but feel frustrated that you can't get it started because you don't have the excess cash to make large contributions, you may need to change your perspective.

What do I mean?

Well, how about getting "addicted" to the habit of saving money on a regular basis, regardless of the amount being saved? Once you get into the habit of saving money, the positive addiction aspect will eventually kick in, and you'll begin increasing the amount you set aside ... and get to your retirement goals sooner!

Research shows that it doesn't matter so much the amount of money saved, the length of time spent exercising, or the number of teeth flossed ... as developing the habit of doing something that you know is good for you and doing it every day, every week, every month, and every year. That is an example of developing a positive addiction!

May I recommend two books that ... no joke ... may change your life! Or at least create some really amazing habits that could very well change your life ... *Tiny Habits* by Dr. BJ Fogg and *Atomic Habits* by James Clear.

In *Tiny Habits*, Dr. Fogg shares the story of how he leveraged the power of tiny habits (positive addiction) to establish a routine of flossing his teeth regularly. He described his teeth as tightly spaced. Ordinary dental floss was shredded and got stuck between his teeth. Over time, it became easier to avoid the entanglement, despite the regular chastisement he would receive from his dentist.

What was his solution? He decided he would floss one tooth a night. That was all he required of himself … one tooth. Oh, and he experimented with over a dozen different dental flosses to find one that would not shred between his teeth. Within two weeks, he was flossing his entire mouth! Boom!! Tiny habits. Positive addiction.

The point? Flossing one tooth barely seems worth the trouble of getting out the floss. But it builds momentum.

For you, it might start with saving ten dollars a week. It's not the amount of money you set aside. It's the action. The amount can be adjusted as you go forward, but the goal is to be addicted to something good for you … saving money!

"Sounds good, R. J., but I have too many days left in the month after running out of money! Even ten bucks a week isn't in the cards … at least not for now."

Well … there's a great saying that tells us to "Inspect what you expect." I think you would agree that saving money is a good long-term strategy. So, if you are left without any funds to set aside, let's "inspect" your finances to see where your green stuff is going.

First … print out copies of your last 3-6 months of bank statements and credit card statements, and look at your ATM withdrawals. Where are you spending your money? If you're a twisted person like me who actually loves building spreadsheets, start posting your expenses to various broad categories to begin to see where you are spending your money.

With ATM withdrawals, it's harder to track … but you can begin to collect receipts for cash expenditures above a certain dollar amount and post those expenses to your spreadsheet. Let's get a clear picture of where you are spending your money, and the longer the period you are looking back over, the better. Six months is better than one. Twelve months might be better than six. But … tiny habits! Tracking even one or two months is better than nothing.

Once you start to get a handle on where your money is going, you can begin to identify areas where you can cut back. And, yes … I know about the $350/month you are spending - and have been spending for 20 years - on that extra storage unit! We are done with that!

Maybe it's time to start watching the home organization shows on YouTube, Netflix, or wherever. Get inspired! Make it a priority to get into the mindset, and you'll start catching the positive fever to cut back, clean up, less is more, and save money!

And, after seeing where you might cut back or defer spending money, what could you do to earn or create more money (hey - I am talking legally here!) Maybe it's time to ask for a raise … or a BIGGER raise (gulp). Or, what about selling some of that stuff in your garage or that storage unit two paragraphs up?

Maybe it's time to ask your friend how they're doing driving Uber or Lyft, or whether you could turn your ability to organize junk into a side hustle, earning a couple of thousand extra a month (or even a week?).

One word of caution: last resort would be selling your spouse's potted plant collection, no matter how much it seems to be taking over the house!

OK … once you have found ways to save money and/or earn more, let's start setting some aside. Remember … positive addiction! It's the habit, not the amount, we're looking for … at least for now!

Set up an automatic transfer from your checking account to a savings account at another institution, such as a credit union. (Lessen the risk of robbing the savings when you overspend!)

And don't worry about finding the highest rate of return for the cash. What rate of return did you earn on your broom last year? (You DO have a broom, don't you???) "Whatttttt? My broom?" Point is … you have a broom that you don't care about the rate of return on it … because you need to have a broom for important reasons. Same thing with the savings … it's important that you build up cash where you can get it for emergencies or opportunities. And you don't especially care about the rate of return. Just build up the cash … and feel great about forming an important, positive addiction!

Ideally, you want to eventually set aside 3-6 months' worth of expenses in cash. Remember the financial pyramid from the last chapter? The more unpredictable your work or income, the more months of replacement income you should build up. I have commercial real estate advisor clients who have 1-2 years' worth of income set aside in cash because of the unpredictable nature of their careers.

The principle of positive addiction isn't just about building your savings … it carries over to growing your assets as well! The more money you set aside, typically, the faster your estate will grow, and you will discover the 8th Wonder of the World! (Pssst … check out the next chapter … "The $100,000 Bonus!")

I get it … it may take some time to create positive addictions. So… while I'm at it, may I share another positive habit to consider? That is, pay cash when you buy groceries or when you eat out. Other places where you would use your credit card or debit card without thinking.

A study done by Dun & Bradstreet found that people spend 12-18% more when using credit cards instead of cash. McDonald's reports its average ticket is $7 when people use credit cards versus $4.50 for cash. It may not be as convenient to carry cash, but there is a pain factor in laying out greenbacks that does not occur when we are using plastic.

One extra word … or two … is keep your receipts! You need to know where your cash is going. Without a receipt, it's tough to track, so keep those receipts and enter them into your spreadsheet that day. Oh, and while you may become totally addicted to tracking expenses, we mere mortals should be good with just doing it periodically … and for just a couple of months at a time.

What about retirement plans at work and supplemental accumulation vehicles, such as life insurance? More on that in later chapters!

The bottom line is you need to know where your money is going. If you don't have a firm handle on that, don't be surprised if you're spending a lot more in various categories than you thought.

Hint: You can also use this strategy to pay down any debt.

Action Items

1. Automate moving some of your paycheck into your savings account
2. Start building up that emergency/opportunity fund with 3-6 months of cash needed to pay monthly expenses

CHAPTER SUMMARY

The $100,000 Bonus

How would you like to give yourself an extra $100,000 with little to no effort? No, this isn't a pyramid scheme. It's the magic of letting compound interest do the heavy lifting.

Major takeaways from this chapter will include:

- One thing successful retirees have in common is that they save consistently
- What are the major culprits of "shiny object syndrome" that stall retirement savings?
- The measurable benefits of starting to save money as early as you can
- What starting even one year earlier can earn you!

The $100,000 Bonus

How would you feel about receiving an extra $100,000 as a retirement bonus? Most of us would feel pretty darn good, and it beats the heck out of a gold watch for sure! (Much prefer my Fitbit anyway.)

This chapter will show you how.

One major characteristic of successful retirees is that they consistently save money over time, in good years and bad. As we talked about in the last chapter, they developed a positive addiction to saving money regardless of the amount. So, how does the positive addiction to saving money tie into a promised $100,000 bonus?

Far too often, I watch people putting off saving money, thinking to themselves, "What's the harm in waiting one more year to start saving? After all, I could certainly use that new (expensive) car I've been putting off buying for so long. And that overseas cruise makes so much sense, given the strength of the

U.S. dollar. And, all my friends are renting in that new building on the harbor downtown. Yes, the rents there are really high, but it sure looks fun, and I'll be with other movers and shakers. Good for networking."

And on and on it goes.

Here's the deal. By waiting just one or two years from setting money aside for future delivery, the difference you're missing out on is not the difference from one year to another – it's the future growth and compounding missed in that last year. *That growth* can be $25,000-$80,000, even $100,000 or more!

According to CNBC, much of the population between the ages of 18 and 34 isn't saving for retirement. Neither are 42% of people aged 35-44, nor 40% of those between 45 and 64.

Plus, according to the Stanford Center on Longevity, Americans are only saving half of what they should for retirement. More than forty percent of single retirees end up with just their Social Security to live on. That's frightening when you consider that the average monthly Social Security check is just $1,413.

Most Americans didn't plan on being poor in retirement. But I would submit that the number one reason for procrastination, or the "why behind the what," is that they were distracted by the bright, shiny objects of a consumptive lifestyle. There would always be a tomorrow to start saving for retirement, but they just never seemed to have the income to get started saving.

"What will it hurt to wait a year to start?" is the usual question. We'll look at the math on that before we finish this chapter, but let's look at a few "distractions" that get in the way.

Where does the money go?

- **Cars.** In 2024, the average transaction price was almost $48,724 and is increasing by roughly 2% per year.
- **Housing.** The rule of thumb is that no more than roughly 28% of your gross income should go toward your mortgage, and 36% or less goes toward all monthly debt. Yet, how many follow those guidelines or even stay well below the limits? Most mortgage professionals will tell you how much you qualify for, and then buyers tend to look at homes within that price range rather than those below it.
- **Eating out.** The average American eats out between 4.2 times a week. From 2015–2016, Americans, for the first time, spent more at bars and restaurants than on groceries. The average household spends over $3,000 per year eating out.
- **Jewelry.** In 2024, people spent, on average, $5,500 on a single engagement ring. This is down from $6,324 on average just three years before. In 2018, the average cost of a single engagement ring in California was $9,809.
- **Vacations.** According to a recent report from Bankrate, the average American will spend $1,984 on a weeklong vacation. Since most Americans don't have $1,000 in the bank, much of that vacation expense will be charged on a credit card at an interest rate of 10% to 30%.

It all adds up. If you have all you need in your retirement accounts or are on track with margins, then spend away! However, since 42% of Americans have less than $10,000 set aside for retirement, as reported by Yahoo Finance, spending money as above means you are sacrificing a comfortable retirement tomorrow by excessive spending today. Instead, what if you started putting something aside today? Even if it's not 15-20% of your income that I recommend, you'll still build fantastic money habits.

Studies show that the number one commonality researchers have found in people who have retired well is that they developed a "positive addiction" to saving money that we discussed in the last chapter. It is not so much how much money is set aside as the act of setting money aside in long-term accumulation that will allow you to retire successfully. The sooner we start, the less time it takes to build up a significant nest egg.

For example, let's say someone, at the age of 25, began setting aside $386 per month. Assuming they earn normal stock market returns of 7%, there would be ~$1,019,000 accumulated by age 65, ignoring taxes on earnings.

If someone waited just ten years and then started saving the $386 per month, beginning at 35, by age 65, they would only have $473,656 – less than half of the accumulation of our eager beaver saver at age 25.

In fact, even waiting just one year before beginning to set aside the $386 per month costs results in over $75,000 in lost accumulation over the last year. $75,000! By simply waiting a year! For perspective, that's only $4,632 contributed over one year, which can turn into $75,000.

But what if you were contributing the max to an IRA? In 2026, that's $7,500 per year, or $625 per month. Starting at age 26 instead of 25 means losing $112,308 ... just in that one year!

Start now. Right now. You deserve that $100,000 bonus for developing great saving habits!

Action Items

1. Are you automating your retirement account contributions?
    a. Yes? Great job!
    b. No? Set it up today, even if it's $10. It will be more over time!

SECTION 3

How Long?

CHAPTER SUMMARY

The Longer You Live, The Longer You Live

Most people assume they'll have roughly the same lifespan as their parents or grandparents. This is very, very wrong! It's also very, very dangerous for retirement planning! We can safely agree that running out of money is NOT an ideal retirement!

Major takeaways from this chapter will include:

- Life expectancy has increased dramatically, but expectations of life expectancy have not
- If you make it to age 73, how much longer can you expect to live?
- Three big things to take away from considering "How Long?"
- Promising innovations in medical science
- Retire TO something, not FROM something

The Longer You Live, The Longer You Live

On January 13, 2012, one of the most famous cruise ship disasters happened off the coast of an Italian island. Many wild theories followed the investigation of the Costa Concordia fiasco, with 32 people killed in the accident. Ultimately, it all boiled down to human error and shallow water in which they ran aground.

Whether it's a ship run aground or someone heading to retirement, false assumptions can have disastrous consequences … one in particular.

There is a clever saying that goes, "The longer you live - the longer you live!"

What makes it so catchy … is that it's true! Over the last hundred years, for example, men's life expectancy has increased by 25 years, while women's has increased by nearly 30 years.

But while life expectancy has dramatically lengthened, individuals' expectations of how long they will live have not. At least, expectations have not yet extended to the point of realizing and planning for how much longer their money will need to last.

Life expectancy is the hidden rock in the shallow waters!

The ship captain might be innocently proceeding using a map that he believes is 99% accurate, only to find he has run aground. While there have been several reasons suggested for why the Costa Concordia skipper was sailing so close to shore, nonetheless, he was not expecting to run aground. He was operating on faulty information ... information that wasn't 100% accurate.

I don't want that for you or me.

As you may recall, one of the Five How Questions is, "How long are you going to live?" So ... when I ask that of clients, how do they respond?

Most, frankly, respond with answers about their grandparents and parents – assuming that their predecessors' longevity (or lack thereof) has much to do with their own life expectancy.

However, let's examine the data from the most recent Uniform Lifetime Table, which the IRS uses to determine the annual withdrawal amount required from retirement accounts based on age.

Let's say we have a group of 1,000 individuals, all of whom are aged 73. What is the age when, actuarially speaking, half of the group will be dead, and therefore, half of the group will still be alive?

Did you guess age 99.5 … cuz that's what the numbers tell us!

Granted, this is a "blended" table – one that includes both men and women. The ladies usually have us men by a few years. The significance, however, is that by age 99.5, half of those aged 73 might be dead, but that means the other half is still very much alive! And it means that our money and income have to last a WHOLE lot longer than many are planning for. The implications are enormous. If we ignore the lengthened life expectancies, it sounds like a financial Costa Concordia to me!

The three big takeaways from "How Long" are:

- We need to have some amount of investment real estate and equities in our portfolios for the rest of our lives.
- We will likely need to pay premiums on our life insurance longer than expected, so that our insurance contracts last longer than we do!
- We need adequate levels of fully funded long-term care insurance (because living longer does not mean we are living healthier lives!)

Bonds, annuities, and cash investments can help to "smooth out" the volatility in our portfolios. We will still need exposure to real estate and stocks, however, to grow over time and stay ahead of the steady erosion of inflation and taxes.

If you are a woman, especially, and assume that you only need income for 15–20 years after you retire, think again! You could easily run out of income from your assets and be left with just a monthly check from Social Security. Scary!

Just remember that your grandparents' and your parents' longevity has nothing to do with your own!

I serve on an advisory board for a wonderful non-profit whose tagline is "Imagine Life Without Disease." Did you know we are exceedingly close to a vaccine to eradicate Ebola and Zika, to name just a couple of killers? With them gone, how much longer will life expectancy be further extended?

Another exciting development is that a San Diego company has discovered how to turn on the body's "kill switch" so that a cancer patient will die *with* cancer (from old age) rather than *from* cancer. And in the meantime, they have discovered the compound regrows hair! Coming to a store near you in about two more years!

Eighteen months ago, I had the pleasure of interviewing one of the doctors who mapped the human genome. He believes that we may be within a generation or two of reaching "stasis" in human longevity. That is, we may soon reach the point where we will ourselves determine how long we choose to live. When that happens, I guarantee it will explode our assumptions of planning, investing, and a whole lot more!

Stop me if you've heard this already, but retiring "from" without a retiring "to" usually ends with a trip to the emergency room from a heart attack or something else really nasty. Purpose prolongs life expectancy … but I am getting ahead of myself! Stay tuned for the chapter called "Life on Purpose and Increasing Your Longevity" (Originally titled, "Why Ballroom Dancing Is Better Than Bingo!")

Action Items

1. Make any adjustments to your original answers to the Five How Questions, especially if you based your longevity on your parents or grandparents!

CHAPTER SUMMARY

Increasing the Odds That Your Money Lasts Longer Than You Do

In this chapter, you'll learn how to minimize the risk of the #1 fear of retirees - outliving their money!

Major takeaways from this chapter will include:

- How a platform/strategy can provide a greater withdrawal of income than is traditionally prescribed - with an improved "confidence factor" of not running out of money.
- What is a "Monte Carlo simulation," and why is it important?
- Removing emotion and maintaining a disciplined approach to long-term investing

Increasing the Odds That Your Money Lasts Longer Than You Do

I have found that as clients approach the reality of retirement, a frequent question is, "How much can I realistically take out of my portfolio without running out of money?"

You've probably guessed the theme by now of…well, it depends! (And not the diaper kind!)

We have a new client that we'll call Tom. He came to us frustrated by the low returns he had received over the 20 years of working with a certain investment group. Quite literally, his annualized return after all those years was just over a quarter of 1%. Total! (Ouch!)

When I first saw it, I thought, "Oh, surely I'm misreading this." But he confirmed, "No, this is how much I've put in, and this is how much I have now."

He wanted to know if we could do better. I said, "Tom, it sure wouldn't take much to do better than what's happened here." I then showed him what could happen going forward at different levels of actuarial certainty, using backtested returns and historical data.

Perhaps you're like Tom. Your returns may have been disappointing over the years, and you aren't sure if you're going to run out of money down the road.

We can't erase what has happened in the past, but by utilizing a platform that takes the emotion out of investing, we can actually increase your withdrawals by as much as 50% more - while still having a "confidence factor" (the confidence of not running out of money!) of over 90%.

As an illustration, the chart below compares three different allocations from our preferred investment platform to the Vanguard S&P 500 Index fund (the 500 largest companies in America and "weighted" to the market value each company has overall) and the traditional 60/40 mix of stocks/equities vs. bonds/fixed income.

We then "stress test" each of the portfolios over 30 years and include a 3% annual Cost-of-Living-Adjustment (COLA). After all that, we determine the statistical probability that there is still money left in our investment portfolio to pay us an income stream!

Running out of money at the age of 85 is not a pretty sight! Running out at age 80? Oh my … far worse!

This statistical analysis has a fancy name. It is called a "Monte Carlo simulation" and, with the aid of lightning-fast computers, runs thousands upon thousands of iterations to determine the likelihood of certain financial outcomes.

VANTAGE 2.0 MONTE CARLO SIMULATIONS | SAFE WITHDRAWAL RATES

Withdrawal Rate	Vantage Conservative 2.0	Vantage Balanced 2.0	Vantage Aggressive 2.0	Vanguard S&P 500	60/40 Balanced Index*
	Probability of success over 30 yr. period with a 3% annual increase				
1%	99%	99%	99%	99%	99%
2%	99%	99%	99%	99%	99%
3%	99%	99%	99%	94%	99%
4%	96%	99%	99%	82%	91%
5%	59%	94%	98%	64%	67%
6%	12%	72%	91%	43%	36%
7%	0%	38%	74%	27%	13%
8%	0%	13%	52%	15%	3%
9%	0%	3%	28%	8%	0%
10%	0%	0%	13%	3%	0%

* 60% Vanguard S&P 500 and 40% Vanguard Total Bond Index

As an example, a 4% withdrawal factor has been considered a "safe" withdrawal rate over the years. That is, historically, someone could withdraw 4% of their portfolio every year with a high probability (a high confidence factor) of not running out of money.

Given the immense volatility in investment markets we've experienced over these last two decades, however, many are wondering if this "safe" withdrawal rate should actually be 3% instead.

3%? That's a bummer!

But there is good news! Huzzah! Using the approach that we considered above and looking back over the last 30 years, we can comfortably make the case for taking a 4% withdrawal with a 3% COLA.

In fact, even at a 6% withdrawal rate and 3% COLA, using the Aggressive 2.0 portfolio, the backtested model has a 91% probability of still having money left in the account after 30 years!

How about the S&P 500?

Using the Vanguard S&P 500 Index (VTI) as an example, there's a 94% probability that your money will last 30 years, withdrawing at 3% and with a 3% annual cost-of-living adjustment. That means there's only a 6% probability that you'll run out of money.

With a higher percentage withdrawal - say 4% with a 3% COLA - what happens? The Vanguard S&P 500 Index drops to only an 82% certainty factor.

At a 5% withdrawal factor (and 3% COLA), the "success rate" drops to only 64%, and only a 43% success rate if we assume a 6% withdrawal and 3% COLA.

Scary!

Contrast those success rates with the 60/40 stocks/bonds allocation and the three Vantage portfolios. How do they measure up against each other?

You can look for yourself, but the 60%/40% traditional allocation does better than the S&P 500 Index if the withdrawal rate is lower. It performs less favorably, however, as withdrawal rates increase.

All three Vantage portfolio allocations, on the other hand, perform quite well up to a 4% withdrawal rate. What is interesting, however, is how well the Vantage Balanced and Vantage Aggressive portfolios do when we increase the rate of withdrawal to 5% and even 6%!

This should be very encouraging news to anyone, like our friend Tom, who has experienced subpar asset growth. You can likely make up for lost time (at least in part) and take a higher percentage withdrawal without unduly risking the longevity of your assets.

Now, you're probably wondering why anyone would choose the Vantage Conservative 2.0 when the Aggressive 2.0 has a higher probability of your money lasting longer at higher withdrawal rates.

Looking at the chart, you might be inclined to think there is no room for using the conservative allocation. However, if you make your assumptions based on the conservative portfolio results while allocating toward a balanced portfolio or a portion into the aggressive portfolio, this could help in your future planning if you want to be ultra-conservative. The likelihood is that it will not perform as subpar as the conservative portfolio if you gradually increase the percentage of equities over time. However, it still gives us a point of comparison to stay with a 4% withdrawal factor, knowing that you could switch the allocation and the percentage withdrawal rate if you need to.

But what if you want to be conservative in your planning approach? For some folks, the volatility of the market becomes so paralyzing that they don't want to put themselves in that position … worrying all night about every blip in the economy. The conservative allocation helps us see that 4% is a comfortable withdrawal amount, but if we need to take more out in a particular year, we can do that, assuming we use a balanced or aggressive allocation!

Now, in reality, very seldom do people opt for the conservative allocation. They either choose to use a balanced allocation or they start with a balanced allocation and switch over to an aggressive one. I've had that happen frequently. And then, there are just people like me who start out in the aggressive growth portfolio from the get-go. Yes, there will be more wiggle, but backtested over 30 years, there is a meaningfully higher return. (Although, once again, "past performance is no guarantee of future results.")

The probability of success in a balanced portfolio over 30 years is 94% at a 5% withdrawal rate. Much higher than the recommended 3%. Even a 6% withdrawal rate has a 72% chance of lasting three decades!

But the aggressive allocation gets even better. Historically speaking, a 5% withdrawal rate gives a 98% certainty factor of not running out of money. Even bumping the withdrawal rate to 6%, your odds of your money outliving you are still at 91%.

Let me repeat that.

There's a 98% probability that your aggressive portfolio will last over 30 years, compared to 64% with the S&P Index and 67% with the 60/40 portfolio, assuming a 5% withdrawal rate!

It also gives you options. If somebody is older or in poor health, they could take a 6% withdrawal with a 3% COLA - something almost unheard of! And they'll have a 91% probability of never running out of money.

For the skeptic reading this, understand that it's due to this approach's dispassionate methodology that we see these kinds of results. Let the math work for itself, and don't try to spit in the face of history.

We have 30 years of data saying, "14 recessions and 30 years later, trust the research. Trust the data."

And Tom, who was worried that he couldn't retire because of his two decades of poor returns? He had a positive addiction to saving money. By course-correcting his strategy, combined with his positive addiction to saving money, things have turned around substantially, and he has started to picture having a mai tai on the beach again!

As long as you're living below your income and putting money away, you have a great start to creating your ideal retirement.

Action Items

1. Based on your current investment strategy, what withdrawal rate have you been assuming? Start by looking at the probability of certainty that your portfolio will last 30 years. Is that enough? Will you have to reduce your percentage withdrawal? If you do, is that enough to meet your objectives?
2. What certainty factor percentage will allow you to sleep well at night? (And your spouse!)
3. Adjust the number on your "How Much?" by the following:
    - **a. 2% withdrawal:** target retirement income / 0.02 = How Much?
    - **b. 3% withdrawal:** target retirement income / 0.03 = How Much?
    - **c. 4% withdrawal:** target retirement income / 0.04 = How Much?
    - **d. 5% withdrawal:** target retirement income / 0.05 = How Much?
    - **e. 6% withdrawal:** target retirement income / 0.06 = How Much?

CHAPTER SUMMARY

Diversifying Income Streams and Sequence of Returns Risk

We're going to cover a very stodgy-sounding topic, "sequence of returns risk," because it applies to the four most dangerous years for your retirement savings you worked so hard to build.

Major takeaways from this chapter will include:

- How "don't have all your eggs in one basket" applies to retirement planning
- Defining "sequence of returns risk"
- The four most dangerous years for ensuring a successful retirement
- What "multiple buckets to draw from" looks like
- The "$1.6 million difference"

Diversifying Income Streams and Sequence of Returns Risk

I bet you've heard the saying, "Don't put all your eggs in one basket."

That was one of my mom's favorite expressions. And, as usual, Mom was right! And guess what? We can apply that same wisdom to retirement planning as well!

"How?" you ask.

Here's how … and it applies to a "risk" that most people have never heard of before … "sequence of returns risk."

Whoa … what the heck is that?

It is a risk that we are exposed to if we draw our retirement income from one primary source. The risk is: What if the returns in that "bucket" turn negative? What do we do then?

"Gee … negative returns … like now?" you ask.

Yes … exactly like what has been happening with the immense volatility (ups and downs) over the last few years … in the stock and bond markets. Yikes!

This risk is best avoided by having multiple buckets of income in addition to our primary income source, whatever that may be right now. Stashing our "eggs" in various places and ideally in "asset classes" that go up or at least remain stable in value when other asset classes are going down.

What else?

Do you know the four most dangerous years to navigate in ensuring a successful retirement? It's the two years just before you retire and the two years afterward.

Why?

Because if you haven't made plans ahead of time to address the "sequence of returns risk" and the economy tanks, you may be forced to postpone your retirement.

Or, the other danger is if you DO begin distributions from your accounts that are down by 10% – 20% – 30% or more, you will likely *accelerate* the collapse of your portfolio!

Not to beat this issue to a bloody pulp, but you get the idea. Right? An ideal retirement requires multiple buckets to draw from as needed, allowing you to retire when and as planned.

What are some examples of buckets that might maintain or even appreciate in value while certain other investments are lying on the floor in a smoldering wreck? (Oh my … aren't we getting dramatic?)

IRA Value When Taking Equal Systematic Payments

Year	Age	Balance At Beginning of Year	Withdrawal	S&P Return 2001-2020	Balance At End of Year
1	65	$ 1,500,000	$ (90,000.00)	-11.85%	$ 1,242,915
2	66	$ 1,242,915	$ (90,000.00)	-21.97%	$ 899,620
3	67	$ 899,620	$ (90,000.00)	28.36%	$ 1,039,228
4	68	$ 1,039,228	$ (90,000.00)	10.74%	$ 1,051,175
5	69	$ 1,051,175	$ (90,000.00)	4.83%	$ 1,007,599
6	70	$ 1,007,599	$ (90,000.00)	15.61%	$ 1,060,837
7	71	$ 1,060,837	$ (90,000.00)	5.48%	$ 1,024,039
8	72	$ 1,024,039	$ (90,000.00)	-36.55%	$ 592,647
9	73	$ 592,647	$ (90,000.00)	25.94%	$ 633,034
10	74	$ 633,034	$ (90,000.00)	14.82%	$ 623,512
11	75	$ 623,512	$ (90,000.00)	2.10%	$ 544,716
12	76	$ 544,716	$ (90,000.00)	15.89%	$ 526,970
13	77	$ 526,970	$ (90,000.00)	32.15%	$ 577,456
14	78	$ 577,456	$ (90,000.00)	13.52%	$ 553,360
15	79	$ 553,360	$ (90,000.00)	1.38%	$ 469,754
16	80	$ 469,754	$ (90,000.00)	11.77%	$ 424,451
17	81	$ 424,451	$ (90,000.00)	21.61%	$ 406,726
18	82	$ 406,726	$ (90,000.00)	-4.23%	$ 303,329
19	83	$ 303,329	$ (90,000.00)	31.21%	$ 279,909
20	84	$ 279,909	$ (90,000.00)	18.01%	$ 224,111

Let's say when you retire, you have accumulated $1.5 million in an individual retirement account. In our example, you begin taking out $90,000 per year. (Normally, I would not recommend taking out that high a percentage—6%—but it just makes the math easier for our discussion.)

Let's also assume that you began taking out your withdrawals in 2001 for 20 years. By the end of 2020, your bucket would be running dangerously close to empty … having $224,111 still available for distribution.

Now, what if, instead, you have two buckets to draw from? You have your IRA and a backup bucket of cash - a life insurance contract designed to be cash-rich and available for supplemental retirement income on a tax-favored basis. (See the Chapter "Life Insurance Bucket" for how this works.)

Let's further change one other thing in our example. Let's assume you take out your $90,000 of income on January 1st each year. And, in any year where returns in your IRA are negative, the following year, take your $90,000 from the backup bucket. During the twenty years from January 1, 2001, through December 31, 2020, there were four years when returns were negative. Not being forced to take income out of your IRA in the years following negative returns and instead giving it a year to recover makes a significant difference.

IRA Value Using Alternative Income Source After S & P Down Year

Year	Age	Balance At Beginning of Year		Withdrawal		S&P Return 2001-2020		Balance At End of Year
1	65	$	1,500,000		-	-11.85%	$	1,322,250
2	66	$	1,322,250		-	-21.97%	$	1,031,752
3	67	$	1,031,752		-	28.36%	$	1,324,356
4	68	$	1,324,356	$	(90,000.00)	10.74%	$	1,366,926
5	69	$	1,366,926	$	(90,000.00)	4.83%	$	1,338,602
6	70	$	1,338,602	$	(90,000.00)	15.61%	$	1,443,509
7	71	$	1,443,509	$	(90,000.00)	5.48%	$	1,427,681
8	72	$	1,427,681	$	(90,000.00)	-36.55%	$	848,759
9	73	$	848,759	$	(34,362.71)	25.94%	$	1,025,650
10	74	$	1,025,650	$	(90,000.00)	14.82%	$	1,074,313
11	75	$	1,074,313	$	(90,000.00)	2.10%	$	1,004,984
12	76	$	1,004,984	$	(90,000.00)	15.89%	$	1,060,375
13	77	$	1,060,375	$	(90,000.00)	32.15%	$	1,282,351
14	78	$	1,282,351	$	(90,000.00)	13.52%	$	1,353,556
15	79	$	1,353,556	$	(90,000.00)	1.38%	$	1,280,993
16	80	$	1,280,993	$	(90,000.00)	11.77%	$	1,331,173
17	81	$	1,331,173	$	(90,000.00)	21.61%	$	1,509,391
18	82	$	1,509,391	$	(90,000.00)	-4.23%	$	1,359,351
19	83	$	1,359,351	$	(83,395.77)	31.21%	$	1,674,180
20	84	$	1,674,180	$	(90,000.00)	18.01%	$	1,869,491

Assumes a hypothetical $90,000/year withdrawal each year in first example.
Hypothetical example for illustrative puposes only. Beginning value of $1,500,000 in an IRA.
S&P historical return during 2001-2020 including dividends.
Source: http://pages.stern.nyu.edu/~adamodar/New_Home_Page/datafile/histretSP.html
In second example, $0 withdrawal in years following a negative return except for the required minimum distribution.
$34,362.71 & $83,395.77 are the required IRS minimum distributions from the IRA for these years.
S&P Index is a list of securities frequently used as a measure of the U.S. Stock Market performance.
These numbers do not reflect fees and costs associated with the actual investment.

How much of a difference? Would you believe a $1.6M difference?

How is this possible?

Because clever you preplanned for that pesky sequence of returns risk. The year after an account has been hammered by the wiggle of poor performance, we let our IRA recover. Instead, we meet our income needs from the cash values of the life insurance contract or a portion of our home equity.

This results in having nearly $2 million in our IRA at the end of 20 years, simply by not taking income out the year following a market downturn.

You clever readers may have noticed in the chart that Uncle Sam requires us to withdraw a certain amount of money once we reach the age of 73. It's called "Required Minimum Distributions" or RMDs. Basically, you will be required to "draw down" a specific percentage of your retirement accounts each year after age 73 … or face heavy penalties.

In our example, we were forced to take income to meet the required minimum distribution even though it followed a negative year in the stock market. Nonetheless, we still come out ahead.

And in addition to investment-grade life insurance or a reverse mortgage, there are other types of assets we can draw from, such as refinancing, investment real estate, Social Security, Health Savings Accounts, annuities, and other asset classes, which we will cover later.

In summary, having multiple buckets (padded!) means that even if the eggs in one bucket are crushed, we don't lose them all. Thanks, Mom! We will take income from whichever account is doing the best at the time that we need it. By taking only three years of income and partial distribution in two other years from our backup bucket, we end up with over $1.6 million more in our IRA at the end of 20 years! Nice job!!

Action Items

1. Are you in a financial position to start building different buckets right now? Like "investment grade" life insurance, paying off your mortgage, or rental real estate income?
2. How can you get there from where you are on the financial pyramid?

CHAPTER SUMMARY

Medicare: What's Going on Over There and What Can We Do About It?

Now that the news has scared us senseless about the future of Medicare, how can you ensure that you can handle whatever medical expenses come your way?

Major takeaways from this chapter will include:

- When is Medicare projected to go into deficit spending?
- How can a Health Savings Account take some of the sting away?
- How likely is it that Congress will push back the Medicare enrollment age?
- How to optimize your healthcare planning coverage in retirement

Medicare: What's Going on Over There and What Can We Do About It?

Just between us friends, no one else is looking, and no one is reporting this to our parents…how many of us really know what Medicare is, how it works, and who it's for?

Most people have some notion that some form of healthcare kicks in when you turn 65. Happy birthday to you from Uncle Sam!

Medicare deserves its own book. It's a doozy! My best advice is to find a professional on your 64th birthday … or perhaps get several *professional* opinions (your uncle, who you only see at Thanksgiving, doesn't count) since nobody seems to agree anyway.

But for our purposes here, we need to figure out how to plan our retirements around Medicare and any potential changes to it before we reach age 65.

Unfortunately, Medicare is in even worse shape than the retirement and disability portions of the Social Security system. For example, Medicare Part A is ***projected to go into deficit spending by 2028!***

Whaaaaaaaaaaat????

According to CBS News, the most likely outcome is that hospitals will either stop accepting Medicare patients altogether or reduce the number of patients they accept. The hospitals will just not be getting enough payment to keep the lights on and salaries paid.

You heard right…deficit spending by 2028. That's just around the corner, folks!

"Just how important is Medicare Part A anyway?" you ask.

It's only the part that covers hospital stays, skilled nursing care, hospice care, and various aspects of home health care.

That's all!

This is major league stuff we're talking about. So far, no one has even come close to finding a solution to save Medicare. Lowering prescription drug costs in Part D is like rearranging the deck chairs on the Titanic. Medicare already provides benefits to over 67.3 million Americans as of 2024, and this number is growing rapidly. Most of those covered are age 65 or older, and holy cow, are they using the benefits.

So what do we do? "Medicare Insolvency Day 2028" will be here in the blink of an eye! And that will not be a holiday.

In Section 4 - Buckets, you will find a chapter on Health Savings Accounts (HSA). The very short version is that it is a wonderfully tax-advantaged vehicle you can invest in and then use for healthcare expenses. If you get your HSA set up and are saving and investing to the max each year, you "should" be OK.

Contributions to your HSA are deductible (at least federally), grow tax-free, and provide tax-free withdrawals as long as you use them for medical purposes! If this chapter doesn't scare you into setting up an HSA by the end, we'll come back to how vital this is for your financial health. (Alternatively, you are welcome to skip ahead, read that chapter, and come back.)

The best thing you can do is talk to an expert in your area about how Medicare works before you get to that stage. In my case, I sat down with my advisor nine months before my birthday to make the necessary decisions.

Now, it's highly likely that Congress will push back the Medicare enrollment age. After all, they've pushed back the Social Security age. Why not make them match?

If benefits do end up being cut, your HSA will help offset some of the additional costs.

However it shakes out, let's prepare to pay more for healthcare. Setting up tax-advantaged vehicles will ensure those costs won't take a T-rex-sized bite out of your standard of living.

We will have to reckon with the Medicare balance sheet as a nation over the next few years and likely revisit it periodically.

It's unlikely you or I can change the system as individuals. But here are some ways to keep yourself and your family able to enjoy your ideal retirement rather than worry about medical bills.

Assume That Medicare Benefits Will Be Reduced.

Remember our suggestion to factor in a likely reduction in Social Security benefits? If you plan with the idea that Medicare benefits will be a pale shade of what they are today, you'll be prepared. Plus, if they aren't, you're in for a happy surprise. Maybe use the extra money in one of your buckets for an outrageous yard ornament, a statue with a waterfall, or a duck topiary!

Get Your Life Insurance Sorted Out Today.

OK, well, maybe tomorrow if you take care of your HSA today (I don't think I'll let you off that easily.) There's an old saying about planting trees. "The best time to plant a tree was 20 years ago. The second best time is today." It works the same for insurance. Locking in the life/disability/long-term care insurance premiums as young as possible gives you the lowest rates. Also, see the chapter "Life Insurance Bucket," where we will discuss using it as an additional source of non-taxable income.

The other part of life insurance is that companies often bundle in, or you can tack on long-term care or chronic care benefits for a few extra bucks each month. This pays the increasingly heart-stopping expense of care in nursing homes, assisted living facilities, and even in-home care.

Fund Your HSA to the Max!

I suppose instead of saying, "I'm trying to sound like a broken record here," (do kids even know what those are?) I want to "stream this song on repeat" until everyone gets on a high-deductible health insurance plan, sets up an HSA, and funds it to the max every year. Even if you have medical expenses and need to use some of that cash this year or next, you'll still be ahead when you hit retirement, and those health costs start ramping up. Plus, who can't use an extra tax deduction (at least federally) for either single or family coverage?

Finally, Check Expected Medical Costs in Retirement Every Few Years, Also Known as Planning Ahead!

Scary fact: The average couple retiring today in the U.S. can expect to spend $315,000 on healthcare costs during their retirement years. That number might not help if you're (very smartly) reading this when you're 25. That's 40+ years of changes to plan for. Hard to pinpoint, considering 40 years ago today, we all thought hair metal and jazzercise would last forever.

In a perfect world, you will start your retirement journey with $315,000 safely socked away in your precious HSA. But if you don't arrive at age 65 with more than $57, what do you do?

It is highly advisable that you talk with a Medicare supplement expert who can help you understand the many choices available today and likely more in the future. I have two vetted specialists who focus exclusively on this area, to which I am happy to make a referral.

Working with health insurance experts and some volunteer resources can help you find the right type of coverage for your situation. Plus, the HSA strategy detailed in Section 4 can help.

I know some of you look forward to planning ahead like getting a root canal. Nonetheless, taking the time to discuss and think through this to develop a healthcare master plan for your ideal retirement is better than the "age 65 with $57 in your pocket" outcome.

Action Items

1. To be conservative, assume Medicare benefits will be reduced before you get there if you're not on Medicare already. (If they aren't, then you have a happy surprise and more money left in your wallet!)
2. Set up your Health Savings Account and High-Deductible Health Plan if you haven't already done so (yes, this will be a recurring theme from now on).
3. Get your "investment grade" life insurance set up primarily for non-taxable income, but also with an ultimately tax-free death benefit.
    a. By the way, did you realize that in some states (Texas, for example), 100% of the money in life insurance contracts is exempt from creditors?
4. Make a note in your retirement plan to Google "expected healthcare costs for retirees" every couple of years. It keeps going up, and we don't want you to be surprised.

SECTION 4

How Many?

CHAPTER SUMMARY

How Can We Solve Social "Insecurity?"

Social Security is struggling financially. What can you do to protect yourself during retirement, no matter what Congress decides to do about it?

Major takeaways from this chapter will include:

- Social Security background – how did we end up here?
- How to check your own Social Security eligibility
- Solutions being considered to address the underfunding of the system
- Join the 5% club to maximize your Social Security benefits

Can We Solve Social "Insecurity?"

Social Security Retirement Income is the first bucket that most people think of when they think of retirement. You hit that magical age of 65 or 67, and poof, the government pays you money each month!

But, wait…

No doubt, you have been in a conversation where someone will remark that Social Security is going bankrupt. (Or you have just had a nasty shock.)

Is that true?

Fortunately, as we'll unpack below, that's not the whole story.

Yes, the original Social Security program was created to be a "pay-as-you-go" model. As said (probably too often), it was not actuarially calculated even at the outset. No doubt, this fact alone perhaps rightly causes cynics to question its longevity.

To make matters worse, Congress has added even more benefits without regard to the actual cost of those enhancements. And now those "chickens have come home to roost." Cock-a-doodle-doo!

For example, in 2022, the Social Security system paid out approximately $1.14 trillion, while only taking in $1.08 trillion in taxes and interest. And guess what? Those benefit payments will continue to increase every year for as long as the maps still show the United States of America.

But here's the deal. The system will only be bankrupt if there is no longer money being supplied to the system via tax revenues and trust interest. And can you imagine the 66 million people presently receiving benefits shrugging their shoulders and saying, "Gee, Phyllis, I guess we didn't really need that money anyway, huh?"

Hello! There would be an upheaval like nobody's business! If you thought January 6th was a rough day for Congress … you haven't seen anything yet if Social Security checks stop coming!

You see, even though underfunded, the programs will continue to receive revenue from payroll taxes. This, in turn, will be paid out in benefits. However, based on current projections, that money won't be enough to cover the program's costs. This is partly because, as trust fund balances decline, the amount of interest that the trust funds earn on their assets will also decline.

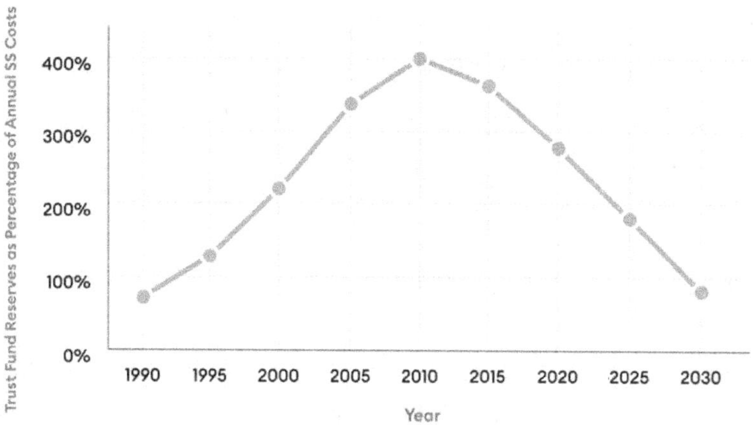

Let's create an analogy here.

You have a lovely property that includes a well with pure water! So, even though there is a drought condition, your well is keeping you well hydrated, and your lawn is nice and green!

The well is fed from an aquifer (a below-ground lake) via underground streams. These underground streams get their water from the rain and runoff from the nearby glacier, which makes your home so picturesque.

Unfortunately, as the glacier melts and the drought continues, there's less and less runoff each year to refill the aquifer that supplies your well.

Eventually, without any changes in weather patterns bringing you more rain and snowpack, your aquifer will be depleted, and your well will dry up. You'll be left with mud and rocks except for whatever rainfall happens to come your way.

And that is what is happening with our wonderful Social Security system. Eventually, we'll just be left with small amounts of water flowing into the system, but mostly mud and rocks.

So, How Do We Fix Things?

The simple solutions have already been implemented or at least attempted, so what else can be done?

In 2018, for example, the Social Security Trustees calculated that the program would be able to provide 77% of benefit payments overall for both disability and survivor benefits, even though we'd be down to mud and rocks. The following year's report saw some improvements along these lines, with the overall figure improving to suggest Social Security will be able to pay slightly more – 79% of combined scheduled benefits.

Fine, but how do actual retirees feel about reducing their income by 21% to help balance the federal budget shortfall?

Anyone out there want to take a stab at the answer?

Short answer: "NO WAY! Read my lips!"

A May 2021 survey by AARP found that 85% of American adults age 50+ strongly oppose cutting benefits to help reduce the federal budget deficit. These feelings, by the way, run equally across the political spectrum.

I think one obvious reason for this strong reaction is that the current payout levels are critical to the financial health of many older Americans. Research shows that Social Security provides the bulk of family income for almost half of Americans age 65 and older. Plus, for a substantial number of retirees, Social Security is THE only source of income.

The sad reality is that most Americans have saved little to nothing for retirement. Perhaps that helps explain why over 50% of Americans have applied to receive benefits when they turn age 62 – in most cases, the earliest age permitted. They do this despite receiving a 30% haircut on the benefits they will receive now, which is also 30% less available to receive annual compounding of future benefits.

OK … so reducing benefits across the board doesn't work. What else can we try?

Here are a few other ways being considered to save money for the system:

- Begin phasing out benefits above a certain income level - so-called "means testing"
- For those still working, perhaps delay the age at which benefits are available
    - Make early benefits start at age 65 instead of age 62, for example

- Begin moving back the "normal retirement age" (NRA) as they have done, moving the retirement age to 67, depending on your year of birth. Why not go to age 68, 69, or even 70 for the NRA?
- Currently, 85% of Social Security benefits are taxable; why not make it 100% taxable, phased in above a certain retirement income level?
- Presently, individuals and businesses are each required to pay the Social Security system 6.2% in taxes on earned income up to $184,500 in 2026
    - Some are recommending that the 6.2% number could be bumped higher
    - Others are suggesting the cap on wages could be raised, on which 6.2% is charged (e.g., pay taxes up to $200,000 and then increase by an annual COLA)
- Some argue that the Social Security system is using the wrong yardstick to measure cost-of-living increases. The current COLA being used measures increases in certain spending areas that don't actually affect those already retired. Switching the annual benefit increases to a different COLA benchmark (a lesser increase) could save billions in payments
- Currently, for every year that a person waits to retire above their NRA, they receive an automatic 8% increase in benefits. Why such a high number? Why not have the deferral of benefits receive an adjustment equal to only 5% or 6%?

Example: If I compare the benefits I could have received starting at age 62 versus waiting until I turn 70, my benefit is 62% higher than if I had begun receiving it at age 62. And, if you are married, not only will you receive a higher benefit by waiting, but so will your spouse, should you predecease them. They can take over your benefit amount. Hence, this feature alone must be costing the system billions of extra payments annually.

Quick tip: Go to the Social Security website and create a "My Social Security" account. That will provide you with useful information, such as the number of credits you have (you need 40 quarters to qualify for Social Security income) and what your monthly Social Security check is likely to be. It may change later, especially if you're young, but it gives you a good starting number on retirement planning as you put together your other buckets!

What If You Are Ready to Start Your Retirement Now?

Unless you have a limited life expectancy, I recommend deferring benefits from Social Security and instead taking income from other sources like your 401(k) or other retirement plans. Let your Social Security benefits grow by the 8% annual COLA until you reach age 70. (After age 70, it no longer increases.)

Not only do you receive a higher amount for yourself, but as stated above, this benefits your spouse. Men are 2.3 years older than their mates on average, according to the math guys and gals. And women typically live longer lives. Taking those two factors into consideration, having those higher compounding benefits can be extremely significant to our better halves! It might even get a foot rub! (Well, at least you can ask …)

Taking money out of your other sources while you wait will be taxable. However, your tax bracket will often be lower. And, assuming you follow our advice in the next chapters and have sources of non-taxable income from your Roth IRAs/Roth 401(k)s and life insurance contracts, your tax brackets may be significantly lower.

Once you start taking your Social Security income, you can reduce your taxable income to levels that potentially make a portion of the Social Security income non-taxable. Below a certain amount, there is 0% tax on SS income. In the next tier, only 50% is taxable, and even at the highest level, only 85% of SS is presently includable in your taxable income.

To Sum Things Up:

I believe the Social Security system will survive (somehow) through:

- Higher payroll taxes on a larger amount of annual income
- Pushing back the age for beginning benefits - both early retirement and normal retirement ages
- A needs-based payment system that would reduce benefits by the amount of other income received from other sources
- Some of the other considerations outlined above

So many Americans are living only on their Social Security benefit that ANY reduction in benefits would hurt those least able to make up the shortfall.

So ... bankrupt? No.

Significantly underfunded and headed for trouble unless Congress acts soon in a bipartisan fashion that is actuarially based? Yes!

One thing is for sure ... those checks are gonna keep coming out! To whom - and when - and how much - and for how long? Well, that's a separate book by itself!

As long as workers and employers keep sending in those payroll taxes, though, and ignoring the mud and rocks ... Social Security will not run out of money!

Action Items

1. Do not factor in any income from Social Security until you're age 70
2. Go to My Social Security (it's a website hosted by the IRS) and check to see if you qualify and what amounts you qualify for at various ages
3. To be more conservative, you may wish to consider multiplying your estimated retirement check by 0.77

CHAPTER SUMMARY

Defined Contribution Ice Cream Plans

It might surprise you to know there are only two basic styles of retirement plans … or, as I like to call them, "Ice Cream Plans." That's it!

OK, some have more sprinkles and whipped cream, some have nuts, etc., but only two basic styles of ice cream plans.

We'll discuss the first type in this chapter—defined contribution plans (also known as 401(k)s and IRAs, for example).

Major takeaways from this chapter will include:

- Quick retirement plan overview definitions
- What type of ice cream plan makes sense for W2 employees
- Benefits of Roth IRAs and 401(k)s
- A major perk for self-employed folks with a Roth 401(k)

Defined Contribution Ice Cream Plans

OK… I've been going easy on you thus far, but now, in this part, I am going to get HIGHLY technical! Ready???

Here it is …

Retirement plans come basically in two forms … "ice cream" plans and "hot fudge sundae" plans.

I bet you're asking yourself, "What do ice cream and hot fudge sundaes have to do with retirement?"

I wish I could remember who to give credit to for these descriptions, but thinking back over my many years of practice and the many different people who have invested in my life … I got nothin'.

But let's cut to the sweet part.

Basically, there are two general styles of retirement plans:

- The first kind: You *know what you'll pay into it*, but have no idea what you'll get out of it at the end!
- Second kind: You *know what you want to get out* of it at the end, but have no idea what you'll pay into it along the way

Let's start with the first kind.

If you walk into an ice cream store, pick your favorite flavor, and say, "Please give me $6 worth of ice cream," do you *really* know how much ice cream you'll get for $6?

You might visually know because the person in front of you just did the same thing. You can go, "Oh, OK, that's my reference point." But you don't really know exactly how much ice cream you're going to get. You're just defining what you want based on what you want it to cost, right?

Well, that's what we do when we put money in a 401(k) plan, an IRA, or a SEP (Simplified Employee Pension). We don't know what we will accumulate in the long term. We just know what we want to put into it based on what we're willing to spend.

Quick Retirement Plan Overview

- Individual Retirement Account (IRA) - An individual account you contribute to and, in most cases, can deduct the contributions from your tax returns. The withdrawals are taxed as income.
- Roth Individual Retirement Account (Roth IRA) - Contributions are made with after-tax dollars, and the money grows and is distributed tax-free.
- 401(k) - Pre-tax contribution dollars are typically set up through your employer
- Solo-K - a 401(k) specifically for business owners (and spouses) with no employees. Otherwise, it follows the same rules as a 401(k).
- Simplified Employee Pension (SEP) - A form of IRA for business owners, allowing contributions up to 25% of their income.
- TSPs - Thrift Savings Plan
- TSAs - Tax Sheltered Annuities
- 457 Plans - for use in the nonprofit world as well … can "stack" it on top of a TSA

Most people start out their retirement funding with a form of ice cream plan… and that's a great place to start! It is important, however, to put away as much as you can, and just funding an IRA/Roth IRA is not going to cut it. (Refer to the chapters "Building a Positive Addiction to Saving" - the

70-20-10 rule - and the chapter "How Much Should You Save to Get There?")

What about you? How much are you putting away? If just in an IRA, that's better than nothing, but have you considered using your employer's ice cream plan (401(k)) to allow for greater contributions? ($24,500 in 2026 with a $8,000 additional contribution if you are 50 or older.)

And, if you're experiencing a sharp pain from answering that question (and assuming you aren't experiencing tachycardia!) … perhaps you feel like you need to be putting more away than you are. You're not sure how *much*, but just a general feeling of guilt that you are not doing more.

Let's just say I understand! I feel your pain! For many years, I was not putting away as much as I felt I should. So, your friend R. J. is here to tell you that there is hope for catching up … and you don't have to wait until you're 87 to retire either!

Let's say you're a W2 employee - what types of ice cream plans make sense to consider? 401(k)s make great sense to participate in.

- This is especially true if your employer (which might be YOU) matches any portion of your contribution
- This does assume you have set cash aside elsewhere for emergencies or opportunities that might arise … ideally 3-6 months' worth of income (see Section 2, chapter "Building a Positive Addiction to Saving")

- Most 401(k)s allow for a "hardship withdrawal", such as pregnancy, purchase/repair of your principal residence, disability, funeral expenses, tuition, natural disasters, etc. However, not all 401(k) plans can be borrowed against
- Additionally, there are limits on how much you can borrow, and typically, you can only have one loan outstanding at a time
- The simple point is … don't cut yourself short of cash and have to borrow money from your 401(k) to bail yourself out

Creating a Roth IRA (or Roth 401(k)) makes sense if you qualify. There are income limits after which you can no longer contribute to a Roth.

- Your 401(k) plan gives you the option to make your contributions as an after-tax Roth contribution
- You won't get a deduction for it now, but the money grows without tax
- When you take it out at retirement, your earnings come out without tax as well!
- You can split your contributions so that some of your contribution is made pre-tax, and the remainder can be post-tax
    - For example, in 2026, your $24,500 401(k) contribution could be split, with $12,500 going into the retirement plan as a deductible contribution and the remaining $12,000 used to fund your 401(k) Roth portion

- In 2026, as said, the limit is $24,500 if you are under the age of 50
- If age 50 or older, you can set aside an extra $8,000/year to "catch-up" in addition to the base amount of $24,500
- The contribution limits increase by cost-of-living adjustments

What this means is that this year (2026), the max for a 401(k) contribution is $24,500, or $32,500, with the age 50+ catch-up provision.

One of the major advantages of a 401(k) - even if you are a one-person business - is that you can deduct the 401(k) contribution from your income dollar-for-dollar. So, the first dollars of income can go into your 401(k), plus there could be an employer match on a portion of your contribution on top of that!

On the other hand, other types of ice cream plans allow you to set aside a percentage of your income. However, they are not dollar-for-dollar programs like the 401(k)s.

The ice cream plans above are good options to create the base layer of your retirement plans. You know how much you're putting in. If you assume normal stock market returns, you have a ballpark figure of where you might end up.

And that, America, is how that works! (I am now leaving to get my $6 of ice cream with nuts and whipped cream. Back shortly!)

Action Items

1. Double-check that you're taking full advantage of any employer match in your 401(k)
2. Are you putting 17% of your income (or up to the max funding) in your 401(k)?
    a. If not, how can you reach that point?

CHAPTER SUMMARY

Hot Fudge Sundae Plans

If you can build a hot fudge sundae plan in addition to your ice cream retirement plan, do it. This chapter will mostly apply to business owners and highly compensated employees.

Major takeaways from this chapter will include:

- How "Hot Fudge Sundae Plans" work
- Know what you'll get from your retirement account decades down the line
- Defined benefit plan explanation & example

Hot Fudge Sundae Plans

So, we've been talking about ice cream plans, with occasional references to hot fudge sundae plans. What's the diff?

Let's pretend today that you want a hot fudge sundae. Maybe you want the nuts, whipped cream, and sprinkles, and of course, you get the hot fudge. Do you know how much it will cost?

Well, if you go there a lot, you might. But generally, no, you don't.

What you are describing is the "benefit" you want. You're focused on what you will walk out of the ice cream shop with. The benefit is the hot fudge sundae with sprinkles, nuts, and lots of hot fudge, thank you very much! What a great country!

This type of retirement program says, "When I retire, I want a percentage of the average of my last few years of income. That way I know that I'll have a similar standard of living to when I was working."

What I'm referring to here is technically called a "Defined Benefit Plan" – the hot fudge sundae. This is the benefit I want to achieve by a certain point in time. There's also a newer version today called a "Cash Balance Plan," but the mechanics are generally the same.

They're set up through the business - or if you own the business, you can set one up for yourself and your employees.

Let's look at an example.

Say you have four physicians. You have one who is five years from retirement. You have another who has three kids in college. They cannot put the same amount of money away because they're in quite different stages in life.

The doctor with three kids in college at the same time may not have the extra cash to put away anything right now, but the doctor who is five years from retirement likely has the extra cash to put the maximum away.

We can individualize the contributions, even though it's the same big plan that's inclusive of all the physicians and, minimally, the staff as well. Primarily, the staff will be provided for through an ice cream plan (also known as a 401(k) Plan), but our physicians in the example will be funded primarily through the hot fudge sundae plan (also known as a Cash Balance Plan).

I put in a hot fudge sundae plan—Cash Balance Plan—for myself several years ago. I've had a 401(k) for years, but now,

I want to be able to put away a lot more for retirement. The Cash Balance Plan allows me to set aside 2-3 times as much money pre-tax as I was putting into the ice cream plan—the 401(k). Yay!

That's all well and good, but how does it work?

First, we need to make assumptions about the rates of return we'll earn each year. Surprisingly, the IRS allows us to be conservative in our investment growth assumptions. In some years, we'll have a negative rate of return on investments. So, to take this into account, the IRS allows us to assume lower rates of return ... even though we hope most years' investment returns will be happily positive.

Understand ... we are not the ones who calculate the returns for our clients in their hot fudge sundae plans. It takes an actuary to perform the actual calculations. The client receives an "actuarial report" that is done annually, which projects returns and a range of other outcomes.

It takes a team of super-smart folks to put those numbers together, not the financial advisor. Our role as the advisor is to recommend investment strategies that will ideally be more predictable year-over-year. This is not the "swing for the fences" type of account, but one where we are primarily looking for "singles and doubles." (Said by the guy who has seen two professional baseball games in my life!)

For example, it is common today for return estimates to be in the 5%-6% range, which is a more conservative number than we might project in our ice cream plans.

Actuaries, by nature, tend to be more conservative anyway. I would say that, with interest rates rising significantly, we may see interest assumptions trending slightly higher. But again, I'm no actuary.

Not only can a hot fudge sundae plan put away a lot more money, but we can often skew the benefit to mainly be directed to the highly compensated – which is often the business owner.

One of our Wealth Legacy Group® clients, with 70-80 employees, was looking for additional ways to reduce their corporate taxes. They had a 401(k) (an ice cream plan) with a nice matching formula to encourage employee participation.

We then looked at overlaying a hot fudge sundae plan on top of the profit-sharing/401(k) plan. Despite having many employees, he was able to direct 89% of the plan contribution towards himself and his wife. Contributions range between $250,000 and $800,000 per year, depending on several factors, such as the amount of taxes he wants to defer and the projected rate of return.

So … if your company is paying too much in taxes, you should consider adding a hot fudge sundae plan to your menu of tax-planning strategies. Let's do it!

And, if you don't have all the cash you need to fund the plan right this minute fully, you can make contributions in the next tax year, and even when on an extension. That means all the way up to September 15th if you are an S Corporation or partnership, or October 15th if you are a C Corp, sole proprietorship, or LLC electing C Corp taxation! And even though it's in September or October of the following year, you can deduct it against income in your previous tax year! Gotta love it!

And, before we go on to discuss the finer points of different buckets and more details of ice cream plans, are you more of a peanut or almond kinda person? Or, no nuts, just more fudge?

Action Items

1. If you own a business, do you have a defined benefit plan?
    a. If not, should you consider one to determine if this financially makes sense for you and your team?

CHAPTER SUMMARY

Exchange Traded Funds (ETFs) and Preventing Disaster

Here's how to minimize the damage a negative market (also called a "bear market") can do to your portfolio. You'll also learn why ETFs (even with inexperienced investors) tend to outperform mutual funds.

Major takeaways from this chapter will include:

- Why ETFs can be better than individual stocks or mutual funds for most investors
- Why investing in entire financial sectors of the stock market is often better than buying individual stocks
- Rebalancing your portfolio periodically, as some sectors do better and others do worse
- "Stop-loss" strategy to limit your losses in a down market
- How much of a return you actually need to offset losses - by percentage
- When to return to the stock market after your "stop-loss" has kicked in

Exchange Traded Funds (ETFs) and Preventing Disaster

Before we get into the rest of the buckets (aka the fun part of retirement planning), I'd like to do a quick detour on an asset you will likely end up holding in at least a couple of your buckets.

Over the last few years, I have become a strong advocate of using exchange-traded funds (ETFs) for many of our clients (me, too!) as opposed to individual stocks or bonds.

Also, I have become less enamored with using mutual funds for several reasons, including overall costs and certain tax issues. Often, we don't have 20 - 30 years of historical performance to refer to for comparative purposes either.

Ideally, I prefer clients to look back over a minimum of 20 years, or longer. This allows us to examine major corrections and how platforms have performed, as well as some of the minor corrections and recoveries in value.

Not only this, but using ETFs also allows us to invest across entire *sectors* of the U.S. economy, not merely high-fliers in technology, finance, etc.

And, speaking of … how about a stumper question for your friends at your next social event?

"How many sectors are there in the entire U.S. economy?"

If you answered with a glassy-eyed stare and a "got no idea," … I was with you until 6 - 7 years ago … and I'm a Registered Investment Advisor! So, no worries!

If you answered "eleven!" (with force and feeling) … then you get escorted to the head of the class! Impressive!

That's right … there are exactly eleven sectors, including two different "Consumer" sectors - one for staples (core items we eat and need - not staples you used to put in your little brother's hand when he was being annoying!) And the other is for discretionary purchases (e.g., the "fun spending.")

Those eleven sectors are:

- Communications & Media
- Consumer Discretionary
- Consumer Staples
- Energy
- Financials (like banks, insurance companies, etc.)
- Health Care
- Industrials

- Materials
- Real Estate
- Technology
- Utilities

Not only do we want a history of at least 20 years or longer to reference for performance, but it is also helpful to invest in an entire sector rather than individual stocks. Why? Investing in an entire sector rather than individual stocks helps us reduce the risk that something cataclysmic might happen to our single stock, which we purchased, and leave us holding a smoking pile of what was once our precious investment.

For example, if we are going to own Chevron in our portfolio, we should also have Shell, Mobil, Texaco, and others because some of those companies may do really poorly for unforeseeable reasons.

Remember what happened to Exxon after that little ship called the Exxon Valdez crashed in Alaska? We watched Exxon's stock value sink like the Titanic, all because they had just spilled millions of gallons of oil on a pristine shoreline. Ouch!

Instead, by using a clever (and low-cost) platform that invests equally across all eleven sectors (to start with, anyway), we can dramatically reduce risk and increase our potential returns. After we make our initial investment, we let the sectors run up or down based on how that particular market segment does. Then, we periodically rebalance the sectors once they reach a certain high or low position relative to the other sectors.

The platform we use offers a feature that you will rarely find, despite its incredible usefulness: a stop-loss. It automatically sells the equity portion of the investment account when the entire "basket" of eleven sectors drops by 10% from their all-time high. It also automatically sells bonds if the fund retreats 4% from its "high-water mark."

The analogy I like to use is this: if you never drive fully into the ditch, you won't have to get pulled out of it. Same thing here. A 10% loss might sting, but it's not like watching your portfolio drop by -36.59% as happened in 2008 to the Vanguard S&P 500 Index fund.

The stop-loss prevents you from catastrophic losses, which also helps you sleep better at night, knowing that your principal is protected.

Then, it automatically buys back into the equity sectors when there is a rebound from the market's bottom. It uses a specific percentage recovery threshold developed from analyzing the fourteen recessions to date since World War II, before reinvesting back into the equity sectors.

The advantage of a stop-loss is that it eliminates the need to watch your accounts daily and check their performance. Having a stop-loss protects your principal before that stop-loss kicks in. It won't keep your account from going negative at times, but it does provide downside protection that isn't there in 99.9% of other investment platforms.

The automatic re-entry provision also takes the worry out of watching your account daily and wondering when you should return to equities. While nothing is perfect, the math behind this exit and re-entry approach has had a positive return far more often than not.

While we are discussing the idea of a stop-loss, I have a question for you …

If your portfolio drops 10%, what percentage return would you need to recover your loss fully? Most people would say 10%.

Great guess … but not quite. Keep reading …

If you have $100 and lose 10%, you will now have $90. If you gain 10% of $90, you now have $99. See what I'm getting at? You'll need just slightly over 11% to get back to where you started … with $100 in your account.

That number only gets bigger the greater the loss the investment portfolio incurs.

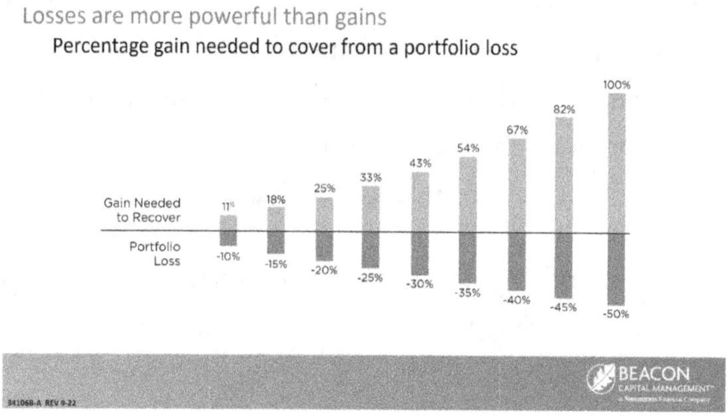

Losing 10% of your portfolio feels awful, but mathematically, it's not too bad. But once you get over 25% losses? You need enormous gains (and years!) to get back to where you started.

Using an emotionless stop-loss that automatically sells when the market takes a downturn and automatically re-enters when certain parameters have been met saves you time, emotion, energy, and, in most cases, your hard-earned money when things are going down. And it usually makes you money while others are still on the sidelines.

This might be a good time to refrain from that oft-quoted saying from our legal counsel, "Past performance is no guarantee of future results!" Meaning that we have to look at the law of averages to be able to make observations.

It's just that without having a stop-loss to give us a parachute when the equity and/or bond markets collapse, it can often take many years to recover from your losses.

As mentioned, no single system or investment approach is foolproof. It's best to look at a 20-30-year mindset for the best outcomes with your retirement dollars. If something doesn't work in a particular year, don't be alarmed if you're using a time-tested strategy. As our trailblazers before us put it, "Don't change horses in the middle of the stream!" (Unless it is a *really* cranky horse!)

There is no perfect solution for every situation. For example, some strategies are not tax-sensitive, such as the platform described above. I will generally use a different platform when the money under management is in an after-tax portfolio. There, the goal is to maximize earnings and growth with as little tax as possible along the way.

With a retirement account—either a pre-tax or Roth account—we're not concerned about the taxability of the assets within the platform. It is a moot point since there are no taxes to be paid on liquidity events inside the retirement account. When the stop-loss does trigger, you will not have a taxable event, which adds "insult to injury,"... paying taxes on gains even though your account has gone down in value.

That's the stop-loss and how it works. It is a fantastic planning tool that most investment platforms do not offer as an option.

Great, Your Money Is Safe. When Should You Re-Enter?

It's one thing to escape the carnage, but then what? When is it "safe" to "go back into the water?" When do you get back into the equity or bond market(s)???

Excellent question. There are those who got out of equities in 2020 after that turbulent first quarter ... and never got back in for the rest of the year! As a result, they missed out on 15%—22% of the increased values that the majority of our clients realized in that year. And, to the chagrin of even certain institutional investment management companies that will remain unnamed ... this was true of them, too.

With the platform we most often use for clients, there is an automatic return feature that has been refined using data from the last fourteen recessions.

This is the clever part.

The longer the downturn (or crash) lasts, the greater the "bounce back" from the bottom that we need to make sure that any gains aren't just a blip. They call it "confidence" in the finance industry.

The buy-back trigger between 0 and 30 days would be a 15% gain from the market low. If the market "basket" of eleven sectors has not reached this figure after 30 days, we then need a 17.9% gain to demonstrate "confidence" that the market has regained its sea legs. At 180 days, we need a 22% gain. Do you see where this is going?

Days Since Stop-Loss Triggered	**Return Needed from Low to Buy Back**
0	15%
30	17.9%
60	19%
90	19.9%
120	20.7%
150	21.4%
180	22%
210	22.5%
240	23.1%

270	23.6%
300	24%
330	24.5%
360	24.9%
365+	25%

The moment the market rises to the required confidence level above the benchmark bottom, the platform automatically buys back into the allocation of ETFs in equities or ETFs in equities/bonds that you were in prior - that is when the stop-loss triggered.

Here's an example of how that would have worked back in the Great Recession of 11/2007 - 01/2009.

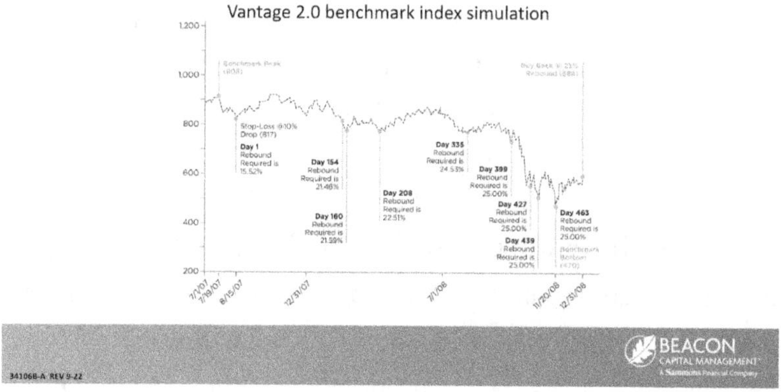

Think of it less like timing the market…remember the old advice, buy low, sell high? Instead, it's about avoiding losses. A 5% or even 10% drop in value will not likely kill your retirement dreams. But, if you're two years away from retirement and the market drops 30%, that quite likely could mean putting off retirement for years just to get back to where you started before the market dropped precipitously.

What I really appreciate about this approach is its:

- Low cost
- Broad diversification across the entire U.S. spectrum of sectors
- Downside protection when the market tanks
- Emotionless investing back into equities/bonds when the market demonstrates "it's time!"

Overall, the automation of the program, with its built-in stop-loss and re-entry mechanisms, allows investors to avoid having to "white knuckle" their way through market downturns. Instead, they can rest confidently, knowing any losses will be greatly minimized. At the same time, there are no "caps" on the upside performance potential of the sectors, such as the caps found in indexed annuities.

Over time, by limiting losses, having low platform costs, and following a sound methodology for re-entering equity markets with confidence … it will allow you to withdraw a higher percentage of assets than conventional wisdom might suggest.

If you are determined to DIY this approach, *Slash Your Retirement Risk* by Chris Cook is a great book on how to do it yourself.

Next, let's get back to all the other buckets you might consider for your ideal retirement portfolio.

Action Items

1. Are you directing your own retirement account(s) and investments?
    a. Are you using ETFs for any portion of this?
    b. Of the eleven sectors that comprise the U.S. economy, how many sectors do your assets represent?
2. If you have assets under management with an advisor, how are they being invested and diversified?
    a. Are they implementing some version of a stop-loss strategy?
3. Read Chris Cook's book *"Slash You Retirement Risk"* (Brilliant guy and a great book!)

CHAPTER SUMMARY

401(k) Bucket

You probably have one (or several) of these. Let's make the most out of it and minimize those management fees that you're paying.

Major takeaways from this chapter will include:

- A great way to accumulate money after building up the Broom Fund
- Consolidating 401(k)s to reduce fees, provide economies of scale, and achieve greater simplicity
- Advantages of moving some or all of your 401(k) to a self-directed IRA for investment diversity
- What on earth is an In-Marriage Qualified Domestic Relations Order?

401(k) Bucket

One of the most popular employee benefits, both today and for some time, has been the retirement plan commonly known as a 401(k) plan. They are nothing more than a form of profit-sharing plan, but one that allows for employee contributions as well as employer contributions.

Fun fact: 401(k)s get their name from the IRS Code section that deals specifically with this kind of retirement plan.

Normally, an employee is eligible to participate in the 401(k) plan after they have accumulated 1,000 hours or more of work for an employer in 12 months, are a W-2 employee, and are not an independent contractor or part of a union.

They are an ideal way to accumulate money ... but, in my opinion, *only* after you have piled up enough greenbacks in a liquid account to cover 3-6 months of expenses if you need it for emergencies or opportunities.

While there are a few "hardship" rules that allow you to take money back out of your retirement account, it is best to have cash building up in your personal savings - your "broom" money. (See this concept in the chapter called "Building a Positive Addiction to Saving.")

Here is how a savings account and a 401(k) are similar: it is not how *much* you put away each pay period, but rather the act of setting money aside. Once you begin to accumulate money in your account(s), human nature is such that you will want to put away more. Positive addiction! Yay!

If you have a 401(k) at work and your "Broom Fund" is built up, we recommend contributing two-thirds of your savings dollars towards your retirement plan, especially if your employer offers a matching contribution (which may be *you*). Anything below the maximum match is lost money, so be sure to contribute enough to receive the full employer match, at the very least.

But what happens to this money when you switch jobs? (Notice the "when" and not "if!" New generation … new norms. Ah, well …)

Since 401(k)s have become increasingly common over the years, it is not unusual for someone to have one, two, or more small 401(k) accounts from a prior employer(s).

Gathering Your 401(k)s

Can you consolidate them?

The short answer is "yes," and it's usually a very good idea to do so. Not only does it make things easier to track, but it can also save money in fees for a stand-alone account once you have left your sponsor-employer.

Basically, you have two options:

- Roll over your predecessor accounts into your new work 401(k) ... once you're eligible
- Or, usually, the better choice is to consolidate your previous accounts into a single IRA, in which you can also roll some or all of the funds into a Roth IRA. (See below ...)

Let's look at both options in a little more detail.

Most employer 401(k) plans offer a variety of fund options, often from well-known "name-brand" mutual fund families. However, their investment options beyond mutual funds and ETFs (Exchange Traded Funds) are limited.

For example, while they may have an investment option for Real Estate Investment Trusts (REITs), they won't have something such as a fractional interest into a real estate private placement (this assumes that you qualify as an "accredited investor" - see the chapter called "Buckets for Accredited Investors") or gold, silver, platinum and palladium coins, bullion or other approved physical forms.

If you are happy with the basic investment forms, rolling your funds into the company 401(k) may be the optimal choice … at least for now.

But, if you want more control over your choice of assets in your retirement account, you can, instead, consolidate your previous 401(k) accounts into a single IRA (but not a Roth IRA). To do this, you should do a plan transfer into the new IRA as opposed to a rollover of accounts.

What's the difference?

A plan transfer can be done every day of the week if you are so inclined. Money moves from one institution (custodian) to another institution. There is no limit to the number of transfers that can be done.

A plan rollover, however, can only be done once per year. In this approach, money is sent directly to you. You deposit the funds, and as long as they are reinvested in the account from which you took the funds - or your shiny, new IRA account - within 60 days … there is no tax on the withdrawal and transfer. However, as mentioned above, you can only do this once per year. The funds must be withdrawn and returned within 60 days, or it will be considered a taxable event. Ouch!

The point is to gather all those loose 401(k) accounts and bundle them all together into one IRA or a variation called a "self-directed" IRA. As the name implies, a self-directed IRA gives you the maximum flexibility for investing in various types of assets.

So, whichever approach you take, get all of those 401(k)s together at the same party.

I recently encountered a situation with a client who had approximately $250,000 in a rollover IRA and roughly $500,000 in a SEP IRA. So, I recommended consolidating the two accounts ... for easier tracking as well as saving some money in fees. It wasn't rocket science, but no one had brought that to his attention before.

In most cases, the administrative fee decreases as the account value increases. While we automatically aggregate different accounts to reduce our advisory fees, most other financial advisory firms do not, from my observation.

An investment sponsor's fee is often reduced as well. Our preferred retirement investment platform, for example, reduces fees substantially once there is $1,000,000 invested with the sponsor. This could be in one account or multiple accounts for a husband and wife, kids, and so on. This is referred to as "householding" accounts for fee reduction, but again, not all sponsors do this; in such cases, consolidate as many accounts as possible. (Pro tip: ask your sponsors about "householding!")

What else? How about doing an "in-service rollover?"

What's this? It's only available if you are 59½ or older, and it allows you to roll money from your 401(k) (NOT you! Don't roll …) and put it into a personal IRA. From there, you can roll money from your personal IRA into a Roth IRA if you wish. Not only that, but having your own self-directed IRA (Roth or regular) offers many more investment options than a typical 401(k) plan allows.

Most Americans today will never have simple lives. But we can certainly try to make our lives simpler. Consolidate your retirement accounts as much as possible.

Is There Anything You Cannot Consolidate?

The only accounts that you cannot consolidate with other accounts are a Non-Spousal Inherited IRA and combining a Roth IRA with a regular IRA.

Inheriting an IRA

Let's look at something called a "Non-Spousal Inherited IRA" for a moment. They have their own unique set of distribution and tax rules as compared with those of a regular IRA.

So, the "bad news" is that we cannot consolidate the assets of an inherited IRA with other regular IRA assets. The "good news", however, is that we can potentially combine asset values in separate investment accounts to reduce the overall fees from the investment advisor and/or custodian.

Important Note on IRAs!

A self-directed IRA and a personal IRA sound similar, but they are not interchangeable terms! They have exactly the same tax rules, etc., but a personal IRA (which requires a custodian, such as Schwab, Fidelity, Vanguard, etc.) is readily available and usually comes with low or no costs.

A self-directed IRA, however, allows for investments in real estate, coins, and other esoteric types of investments. Because there is much more specialized reporting to the IRS involved, it requires a much more sophisticated and therefore expensive type of IRA custodian.

A Huge Advantage with Self-Directed IRAs

One major advantage is that a personal IRA or self-directed IRA can have a greater selection of investment choices than their 401(k) sponsor.

Additionally, an investor can access platforms like the ones we use, which provide a built-in stop-loss in case the market becomes overly frothy.

In short, 401(k) plans do not provide "downside protection" for employees, unlike individual investors who have an automatic stop-loss feature available. And, 401(k) plans are frequently pretty generic as far as available investment options.

In addition to that, "self-directed IRAs" can often include different kinds of asset classes that 401(k) sponsors do not have on the menu of investment options - so-called "alternative assets."

For example, you could hold:

- Real estate investments as a limited partner in:
  - Apartments
  - Senior housing
  - Self-storage
- Private equity
- Precious metals, including gold, etc.
- Coins (American Eagles, but not Krugerrands, for example)
- Crypto
- Collectibles

All different areas in the real estate world that can make sense but are not available through 401(k)s.

I advise any client who is older than 59.5 to consider moving all or at least some of their 401(k) money to their own self-directed IRA. You can transfer funds to your own self-directed IRA, continue to participate in that same 401(k), and receive any matching funds you are eligible for.

Note: There are limits on how much of your IRA funds are considered creditor-exempt depending on which state you live in. Some states, like California, restrict the amount of funds in an IRA you can keep away from creditors. 401(k) accounts or other pension accounts are exempt from creditors. (Check out the O. J. Simpson trial and his NFL pension if you want to read more about the creditor protection given to pension and profit-sharing plans!)

For Couples Under Age 59.5

What about if you have a meaningful amount of money in your employer's 401(k) account but are not comfortable about the amount there … or the lack of variety in their investment menu … and are not 59.5 and eligible for an in-service rollover? Do you have any options?

As a matter of fact … you do!

This next concept was created by a wonderfully creative attorney from Louisiana who discovered a strategy "hiding in plain sight." His name is Marcus Foote, JD, and I want to give him credit.

It's called an In-Marriage Qualified Domestic Relations Order.

Normally, QDROs are used in divorce. They say, "Okay, we're getting divorced. You're getting half of my retirement account. Boom. Here you go."

The lightbulb came on when Marcus realized we could use this tool for happily married couples as well! Someone who has a large account balance of $500,000 or more could hire Marcus' firm, go to the local judicial system wherever they live, get permission from the judge to transfer money out of their 401(k) into a rollover IRA, but in their spouse's name. And there you go!

It allows you to move money out of your 401(k) into an IRA. There, you can then invest with those sponsors that provide a stop-loss feature with automatic reinvestment back into the market when certain conditions are met.

What are the downsides?

One of the key considerations is to ensure that you have a solid marriage, as you are placing the assets in your spouse's name.

In-marriage QDROs have about a 97% "success rate"... that is, the local judge will approve the transaction. Marcus tells me that there have only been a handful of situations where the local judge refuses to allow the QDRO to be used for a non-divorce situation.

It's a very clever idea. It gives people the opportunity to move money out of the 401(k) into a protective environment that they can self-direct. We have personally helped clients grow millions of dollars in accounts like this. It is especially useful with money in tax-deferred buckets, where we then use strategies as described in prior chapters that provide asset value protection when markets drop unexpectedly or suddenly.

One last point ... it would be wise to know if your 401(k) plan allows for "participant loans." These let you borrow from your 401(k) up to $50,000 or 50% of the account balance - whichever is less.

Yes, you do have to pay interest on the loan, but guess who you are paying it to? Yourself!

These short-term loans have advantages over borrowing from banks – lower interest rates and no impact on your credit rating. You have five years to repay the loan. Unless you're using it to purchase your primary residence. Then, you have 25 years!

They're fast, creating an emergency bucket or capital for opportunities (like we get into in the chapter "Real Estate Income Bucket"). Just make sure you pay the loan back on schedule!

Action Items

1. Take your max employer 401(k) match (or if you ARE the business owner, make sure to maximize the business match on your own contributions)
2. Consolidate your 401(k)s to avoid fees
3. Take advantage of in-marriage QDROs (with your wonderful spouse!) to obtain more investment options of your choice, and that can give you downside protection when investment markets turn negative!

CHAPTER SUMMARY

Annuity Bucket

Today, some will say annuities deserve a book of their own! They can get complicated really fast, so we'll just cover the basics - the pros and cons - and how they're taxed.

Major takeaways from this chapter will include:

- Annuity basics - immediate vs. deferred, single life vs. joint life, taxation of, etc.
- Fixed annuity explanation
- Variable annuity explanation … and opinions
- Indexed annuity explanation
- Why an annuity might make sense today for at least a portion of your assets
- How annuities are taxed

Annuity Bucket

OK … I admit it. Until about three years ago, I have been a hater … of annuities, that is!

Not sure when it all started. Maybe I had a bad experience in kindergarten or earlier … but have just not been a fan over my professional career. That is, until advisor friends, who are much smarter than I, have disabused me of my negative thoughts about the financial instrument known as annuities. I have now come to the place of acknowledging that they can play a very useful role in many situations. So … there you go!

Frankly, in these unstable financial times of late, annuities have come up more and more as a topic for consideration in retirement scenarios. I don't know if they are right for you, but let's have a conversation about them and consider how, if, and where they might fit.

The legendary National Football League coach Vince Lombardi is attributed with saying at the beginning of the Green Bay

Packers training camp, "Gentlemen, this is a football." Bringing things back to basics! Everything starts with understanding the basics, and annuities are no exception.

"Ladies & Gentlemen, This Is an Annuity"

It's the systematic liquidation of principal and interest to last over a lifetime.

To begin with, there are ultimately only two basic types of annuities. That's it:

- Fixed return - as established by the insurance company
- Variable return - can either use mutual funds (thus, no upper cap on earnings but no downside protection against negative earnings), or investment returns tied to an index (which generally will have an upper cap, but a downside "floor" return - 0%, commonly)

Not to complicate matters further (too late!), but annuities also come in two options: immediate or deferred. With an immediate annuity, you put a million bucks (or however much) in, and you immediately get an income stream.

A deferred annuity lets you put money in, sometimes over years, and it grows, grows, grows, and then boom, you get an income stream later on.

The deferred/immediate and fixed/variable create the base of annuity types. But it wouldn't be a whole industry unto itself if there weren't hybrid annuities and then combinations of hybrids creating enough variations to make one quite dizzy!

And that's not all!

There are also single-life and joint-life annuities.

A single-life annuity will pay out for the rest of your life. A joint-life applies to a couple. It keeps paying out after the first spouse dies for the rest of the life of the second spouse.

What about the taxes?

- Annuities inside a retirement account will be taxed just the same as the rest of your retirement account
- If you're taking out just the earnings but have not annuitized the contract, it's all taxable
- If you've annuitized the contract, it becomes a systematic liquidation of interest over a fixed period of years or your lifetime. The portion that represents your original contribution will be non-taxable

So … are you getting a general feel for what an annuity is - or isn't - in the big picture yet?

It might be helpful if we do a quick "fly by" of the building blocks of annuity.

Fixed Annuities

A fixed return annuity is most commonly compared to a bank Certificate of Deposit. It pays a rate of return that is guaranteed for a period of months or years.

People often use this type of annuity in retirement planning when they want a guaranteed income stream. It is often described as a "periodic payment of principal and earnings to last a lifetime." It can have certain guarantees of how long the contract makes payments, even if the initial annuitant (person receiving the money) dies before receiving all of their original investment back.

It is particularly helpful when a retiree is likely to outlive others – that is, because of various factors they anticipate, they are likely to have enhanced life expectancy. In such situations, the annuity continues to pay out as long as the annuitant remains alive. And, with the remarkable extensions occurring in life expectancy, having an annuity that guarantees paying you for the rest of your life could be your single greatest investment ever!

Variable Annuities

Variable annuities, on the other hand, have multiple options for various fund families and fund sub-accounts. For this reason, it is a much more complicated instrument and requires a very sophisticated platform to support the product.

It has two phases. First is the "accumulation phase." This is when you make the contribution, and the money grows (hopefully!) The second phase is the "income distribution phase," which may or may not involve actual "annuitization."

Notably, considering all the options and the requirements of that sophisticated platform, variable annuities can also be significantly more expensive than a simple fixed annuity.

It's not unusual to see a variable annuity with an "expense load" of 3% - 3.5% each year. That's quite expensive when you consider the significantly lower return environment we've seen over the last few decades. Most financial resources are projecting returns of just 6.5% - 7% in the equity markets, including the "Oracle of Omaha" himself, Warren Buffett. Subtracting a 3% expense factor from 6.5% - 7% doesn't leave much for the investor.

On top of the expenses for the product itself, there is also no downside protection on variable annuities. In other words, they do not have a floor return. If they lose 17%, you lose 17% of your principal and have to pay the maintenance fees.

While few of us, as financial advisors, are independent Registered Investment Advisors (RIAs), there are increasingly more options for a lower-cost variable annuity contract. There is no cost to enter or exit the RIA variable annuity contract. Zero. And, the recurring fees for various features are typically lower as well.

Considering all these factors, I believe there are often better alternatives available today that are less expensive and still yield respectable returns. If, and that is a big "if," I am going to recommend an annuity for a client, I will recommend considering an indexed approach due to its significantly lower cost and its downside protection of principal.

To me, the greater overall annual cost of a variable annuity is a major drawback. But, it is the lack of downside protection on variable annuities (or other pure equity investments) that is downright scary in the volatile investment world in which we live.

Investing in equities and/or bonds, we will experience years with negative returns from time to time. However, a loss of 4%, 7%, or even 10% over a year will likely not prevent you from achieving your retirement goals. And this is especially true if there are enough good years to have the opportunity to earn +21.7% (the S&P Index return in 2017), +26.3% (2023), and +31.5% (2019), as we have seen in just the last decade.

Here is the point: a -37.0% loss (the S&P 500 Index in 2008), a -18.1% loss (2022), or a -22.1% loss (2002) over a year will take *years* to recover from, if ever. I have had friends planning for retirement who, when the 2008 market crash occurred, and given their aggressive allocation without a stop-loss, had to remain working for another decade to recover from the losses in that single year.

I think of it like falling on a long staircase. If you trip and fall while going *up* the stairs, you might scrape a shin or bruise a shoulder. You'll probably feel a little embarrassed and perhaps shaken, but you will likely be fine.

If you trip and fall going *down* a long staircase, however, there is a serious chance that you may never get back up again.

So, like building codes in the U.S. require handrails on staircases, downside protection on an annuity (or, as we've discussed, on other types of investments) helps to prevent the *really, really bad* falls from occurring.

I want to have my cake and eat it, too. I want (for myself and our clients) to have downside protection while also having no upside cap. Unfortunately, with a variable annuity, I have never seen any downside protections, at least not in commercially available annuities.

This, therefore, leads me to suggest an "indexed annuity" for those who want exposure to equity markets but with a downside stop-loss. So … let's look at that next.

Indexed Annuities

In indexed annuities, your returns are based on an index. (Duh!) That is, we use one or more of the popular indexes out there to measure our rate of growth (or loss). By far, the most common choice is the Standard & Poor's 500 Index, which tracks the

500 largest companies in America. But you might have the S&P 500, NASDAQ, and NIKKEI in your annuity account. For simplicity's sake, we're going to keep our examples with a single index.

Typically, indexed annuities have a minimum return floor. Most often, that floor return is 0%. This means that despite how much of a loss the benchmark might show in that year (say -18.1% as in 2022), your account will receive a "credit" of 0% return.

Hurray, so far.

But just as there is a floor cap that you cannot lose money in a year of negative returns, there's a ceiling on indexed annuity returns as well. Meaning that if your annuity is using the S&P 500 Index as its measuring stick, and it grows by 17%, and your cap is 10%, you will only get a 10% return … not 17%.

Awwww …

Those ceiling thresholds have been quite low over many years, with interest rates hovering just above 0% in the U.S. economy. Now, however, as interest rates have risen dramatically since 2022, the ceiling thresholds have also increased.

Great!

Just how do they measure the rise or fall of the index?

Annuities that use an index benchmark measure the returns by what's called point-to-point. The first point is when you initially put the money in the contract until a later point of measurement, which could be one month or 12 months. In short, they measure the return from the starting point to an ending point with some cap or limit that we described above.

Other Drawbacks to Annuities You Should Keep in Mind

When that money comes out, the earnings are taxed as ordinary income and not long-term capital gains with a more favorable tax rate, as it would be with stocks, bonds, etc. If you purchased the annuity, however, with after-tax money and annuitize the contract, a portion of the income will not be taxed. You are receiving back a part of the original investment money … which is, of course, not going to be taxed. After all, you have already paid taxes on the principal!

But if you have purchased the annuity inside a retirement account, then the income paid out is all fully taxable as ordinary income.

It's a trade-off. It depends on the tax rates of your income during the accumulation phase. You might be able to grow a substantial amount of money without having to pay any taxes along the way. That can be attractive.

That's one thing to bear in mind. The other one, of course, is what tax bracket you expect to be in when you begin taking withdrawals. Would you be better off taking withdrawals from a stock portfolio where your taxes will be long-term capital gains instead of ordinary income? However, your income stream might be low enough that the difference in tax brackets is not significant.

One more item for consideration is the tax concept of LIFO - "last in, first out." Meaning that any withdrawals taken will be fully taxable because the last money going into the account is considered tax-deferred earnings.

However, if you are fortunate enough to have purchased an annuity before August 14, 1982, it is eligible for FIFO … or "first in, first out." For example, if you were to put $1 million in and it grew to $2 million, with FIFO, you would be able to withdraw $1 million. Wouldn't it be great if you were paid that contributing million dollars first because there's no tax? Then you're only paying tax on the second million of growth.

Another common complaint is that annuity payments remain constant and erode over time due to inflation. It is now possible to add a feature that provides an adjustment for inflation. There is, of course, a cost associated with that, and it could reduce early income, but it is certainly something to consider.

Finally, perhaps the biggest complaint (although there are many pros and cons, but we don't want to force you through another 100 pages) is the "surrender fees."

If you surrender (the fancy term for returning your annuity to the insurance company), you may owe the company money for essentially breaking the contract. Because these contracts are rather "commission-rich," the insurance company has to protect itself against exposure should the client want to surrender the contract soon after making the purchase.

To protect the acquisition cost, which typically includes a not-insignificant commission to the writing agent, the company puts on a surrender charge. In short, the longer the contract, the less the surrender charge seems to be. It's not uncommon for surrender charges to apply for 10 years, reducing slightly each year. However, contracts that pay a higher commission tend to have either a longer surrender charge period or a higher charge over those years rather than a decrease every year.

Why Might Someone Choose an Annuity Despite All of the Downsides?

It could be a situation where you want to know you're getting X dollars a month for Y many years. In that case, you might look at a specialty annuity called a "single premium immediate annuity." You contribute a lump sum of cash into an annuity contract, and the insurance company guarantees a specific payment for a defined period of time. That period could be your entire remaining lifetime.

Knowing you have a stream of income, no matter what, can be very comforting.

What if you don't need the income now, but will in a few years or at a certain age? In that case, you could buy what's called a "single premium deferred annuity." A deferred annuity allows you to start the income stream later (I know ... duh!) and also allows the account to grow by some factor. Then, for the rest of your life (or a specified number of years), you'll get an income stream that you can count on.

One of the big advantages of all of this is that the money grows tax-deferred and is only taxed when you take it out.

Final Thoughts on Annuities

If you don't need the income right away, it is best to let the annuity grow. But when you're ready for that income stream, whatever you do, annuitize the contract! It's an easy call to your annuity contract company. That will minimize your taxes and make your money last longer.

And, in case it's not complicated enough, the SECURE Act 2.0 requires annuity holders to annuitize their contracts starting at age 73 – same as the Required Minimum Distribution rules we've talked about.

By the way, when you're ready to begin that income stream from your annuity, there is a special section of the IRS tax code you should be aware of!

Let's ensure you're getting the highest income possible by conducting a comparison shopping exercise. We have over 200 companies, for example, in the annuity space, and many offer multiple options depending on the individual's needs, duration, age, and other factors. If we find a company offering a better contract for you, you can simply exchange the old one for a new one.

You can, instead, evaluate a 1035 exchange, moving your annuity from a better growth/accumulation company to a company with a better income payout schedule. Using an IRC Section 1035 exchange is a tax-free exchange if you find something better!

To wrap up, there are situations where an annuity could be helpful.

- The security of knowing that you're going to receive an amount of income every month, no matter how the equity markets are doing
- You have fixed expenses and want the peace of mind knowing they're covered
- Regular, reliable payments
- Tax-deferred growth if you have income from other buckets

Given elevated interest rates today, if you've never considered an annuity, now might be an ideal time. We may never see another time when annuity rates will be this good. While it's not helpful if you're trying for a new mortgage or a car loan, it's a terrific time to earn higher rates of return with little risk.

Apart from the ravages of inflation, you know that the income stream will be there. That peace of mind is worth something.

Confused yet?

Here are the questions that can help you determine whether an annuity is a sensible option for you.

1. Do you prefer a fixed return, or can your other buckets cover a variable return?
2. When do you want the income stream to start?
3. Do you have a lump of cash that can make a single contribution, or will you pay into the contract over time?
4. What is your risk tolerance?

Action Items

1. Calculate/revisit your likely fixed expenses in retirement
2. What would an annuity cost to cover those fixed expenses?
3. Evaluate if it is worth the cost of an annuity or if you would rather depend on the income stream from your other asset buckets.

CHAPTER SUMMARY

Health Savings Account (HSA) Bucket

You NEED one of these. It's non-negotiable. If you take nothing else away from this book, it should be the Five How Questions. If you take two things away, make it the Five How Questions and setting up a Health Savings Account.

Major takeaways from this chapter include:

- Why virtually *EVERYONE* should have an HSA
- The perfect financial benefit arrangement - deductible contribution, tax-free growth of assets (inside the HSA), non-taxable withdrawals
- What are the IRS requirements for setting up an HSA?
- What are the benefits?
- What features to look for in an HSA

Health Savings Account (HSA) Bucket

If I were to design a perfect financial benefit arrangement, I would want to get a deduction for my contribution to the program, have it grow without tax, and then have the withdrawals all be non-taxable. Brilliant!

Oh … that exists already. It's called an HSA - or "Health Savings Account." (Still brilliant!)

There are a few requirements …

- You have to be younger than 65, because that is when Medicare starts in America
    - You can no longer fund it once you become eligible for Medicare
- You need to have a "high-deductible health insurance plan"

- To be considered a high-deductible plan, however, the deductible only needs to be $1,700 individually or $3,400 for a family (2026)

Congress, in its effort to enable taxpayers to meet ever-spiraling healthcare expenses, created a tool as I wished for above. In 2026, a taxpayer can contribute $4,400 per adult or $8,750 for family coverage. If you're 55 or older, you can add another $1,000 per spouse to that contribution. (For any plural spouses out there, sorry … you only get to count ONE spouse for your contribution!)

When you take the money out to pay for any kind of health expenses - medical, dental, vision, anything related to health costs - it's not taxable.

What's even better is that you can carry whatever has been accumulated in your account forward on an unlimited basis. However long it takes you to spend it all, that's just fine with Uncle Sam.

This is as opposed to a Flexible Spending Account (FSA), which requires an employer to sponsor the plan. And, you are required to spend down all but $680 (in 2026) of your account each year that you fund it. (We refer to this as a "use or lose" provision.)

Additionally, you can only fund FSAs up to $3,400 through payroll deductions. About the only better aspect is that you CAN have a low-deductible healthcare plan, however, and still have the FSA. But, given how little the deductible needs to be for an HSA, that is hardly an advantage for the FSA limit.

But back to HSAs…

Planning Tip

What some folks are doing now (not very many yet, but it's gaining traction) is paying for their expenses out of pocket (anything above 7.5% of Modified Adjusted Gross Income, aka MAGI, is deductible) and leaving their money in their HSA. It grows tax-free and comes out tax-free for healthcare expenses. There's going to be a whole lot more health expenses as we get older.

Many brokerages that provide HSAs will let you invest the money, too. So you can grow it through investments over time, well beyond each year's contribution limit.

Nice!

Not only that, but let's say you haven't filed your tax return for last year because you have until October 15th to file the individual return on extension. You can still set up an HSA now (on or before October 15th) and deduct it from last year's taxable income (assuming you have a high-deductible healthcare plan).

It's the only type of contribution or deduction that I know of that allows you to fund it in the following year and still claim a deduction for the previous year in most cases.

One note on tax deductions … some states (like California and New Jersey) treat HSAs as regular financial investment vehicles, meaning you don't get tax deductions for HSA contributions, AND the states tax the earnings inside the account, but only if realized. Interest or dividends earned in the account must be added to MAGI. (MAGI being the fancy term for how much you've made that year.)

If the employer contributes to an HSA, that also gets taxed as income. It's still better than not receiving the additional contribution, but holy cow … yet another reason to leave Cali!

But, HSAs are, in most states, deductible both from state and federal income. The growth is non-taxable (again, in most states) while it grows, and likewise when it comes out (assuming it is used for healthcare expenses). The perfect planning tool!

What Do You Look For in a Great HSA?

Well, let's unpack that question.

First of all, what features does it have? And, OK, what does that mean, exactly?

What you want to look for is a wide variety of options and convenience.

- Is it easy to make contributions?
- Does it have an easy-to-use website to answer your questions?

- Can you easily add money to the account (by linking your bank or other financial source for funds)?
- Is it easy to withdraw funds to reimburse for out-of-pocket expenses?
- Does the custodian give you a card to make payments easy at your medical care facilities?
- Do you have a full suite of investment products and options to help you grow your money?
- Are the reports and statements understandable and easy to access?

The HSA we use is through one of the big players in the investment world. There's no cost for the account. They give you a credit card that basically lets you walk in and hand it to your healthcare provider, whether that's a physician's office, dentist, or optician. They take your copayment directly from the card, just as if it were a regular credit or debit card.

They provide the card, account, etc., for free because they hope that we will park the money there for 20, 30, or 50 years until we need it. At that point, they've more than covered the cost of providing the account through the management fees they collect from the mutual funds held in the HSA.

On our end, we need to ensure that diverse investment options are available, as the HSA can accumulate tens of thousands, if not hundreds of thousands, of dollars over time. Those options allow you to invest the money once you have it in there over a certain amount.

The investment options work similarly to those found in managing your 401(k) or IRA. The major companies hosting these hope that you're going to invest the rest of your money with them once you're using them for the HSA. You have a full range of investment options.

You Need an HSA, No Excuses

You may have noticed that Health Savings Accounts come up frequently in this book. And they should! They're brilliant tools. (Yes, I know I keep saying that.)

But here's an example.

According to the 2023 Fidelity Retirement Survey, the average lifetime healthcare cost in retirement was $315,000 for couples. That breaks out to $150,000 for men and $165,000 for women on average.

Let's pretend you're 40 years old and you start an HSA today. If you put in $4,400 every year ($366.67 each month) until you're 65, you'll end up with $297,776.47. That's at a modest 7% compounding interest rate. (Aren't interest calculators fun?) By the way, this ignores the usual cost-of-living adjustment (COLA) and the additional $1,000 we can add each year starting at age 55. Pretty great!!

By contributing a total of $110,000 over the next 25 years of life in our example, you would nearly triple your money. You also statistically have your healthcare costs covered … depending on how inflation and medical costs change over the coming decades.

Clever you!

Now, set a marker on your calendar to adjust your health insurance, whether that's at your office's next open enrollment or when national open enrollment rolls around in November.

Action Items

1. Forgive me for "beating this horse to death" (no actual horses were harmed in the making of this book!)
2. Set up a High Deductible Health Plan (only a $1,700 deductible in 2026)
3. Set up a Health Savings Account with one of the full-feature sponsors out there
4. Fund it to the max!
5. Smile and feel enormously self-satisfied for doing something so tax-smart and beneficial!

CHAPTER SUMMARY

Life Insurance Bucket

Sleep through or skip this chapter at your own risk! We're not going to talk about your "normal" life insurance in this chapter. Yes … it has "four tires and a steering wheel," just like any "financial car," but the engine is supercharged! There is an important reason why this life insurance design is called "investment grade" life insurance.

Officially, you're protecting your wealth. Functionally, you're building a potential retirement income stream where you can turn the spigot on and off as needed … and there is no tax on the income stream!

Major takeaways from this chapter will include:

- Why does "investment grade" life insurance make sense - for whom - and in what circumstances?
- Why the "income stream" is non-taxable
- How you're protected against creditors in many states, as well as bankruptcy
- How this vehicle compares to funding a 529 plan for education
- How and why the life insurance contract builds cash value
- Buy your insurance from a credentialed advisor (such as Chartered Life Underwriter, CLU)

Life Insurance Bucket

Life insurance contracts and their structure have matured and blossomed dramatically over the years. They have morphed into instruments that make sense to allocate a portion of your portfolio.

Using an "investment grade" life insurance contract provides a supplemental retirement income stream, education fund, estate liquidity, funds a buy/sell agreement, helps provide a downpayment towards a home, or even creates an emergency/opportunity fund.

In the not-too-distant past, life insurance was merely an exercise in buying the most for the least. That is, how could we purchase the most life insurance possible for the least amount of premiums?

Whereas today, for many successful individuals, life insurance is more about minimizing the survivor benefit and, instead, maximizing the amount of contributions … the exact opposite of how purchasers of life insurance considered the transaction 1-2 generations ago.

It may sound counterintuitive, but for many high-net-worth and/or high-income families, the point of life insurance is not (just) about the survivor benefit. Instead, it is about building up assets inside the contract, which is free of income and capital gains taxes. And, when properly designed, the money comes OUT without income or capital gains taxes, too.

An experienced insurance advisor will design the contract so that you have the least amount of survivor benefit that the IRS allows and, instead, have the bulk of the cash building up in the contract values.

The cash value in the contract gives us money to draw upon if needed for an emergency or opportunity. Those times do come, and usually when least expected. We want the money to be out of reach, however, so that we're not tempted to spend it needlessly, but still accessible if we truly need the cash.

And, when you open the income spigot in your retirement years, the income will also be without tax (assuming the contract was properly designed in compliance with IRS regulations). An added bonus is that the income will not bump you into a higher tax rate or cause your Medicare premiums to be increased, etc. Lots of things to like here!

Before we go any further, I can almost hear some of you objecting to what I'm saying because your only reference point is permanent life insurance in the form of a "whole life" contract design.

Nope. This is not the kind of contract design I am referring to.

> **Whole Life:** Fixed premiums with a guaranteed survivor benefit. The cash value grows at a set rate, which usually means "very slow."
>
> **Universal Life:** A flexible policy in which you can adjust the premiums and survivor benefits, sometimes called "adjustable life." The cash value growth depends on the contract parameters, usually tied to a specific portfolio or index.
>
> **Variable Life:** Similar to universal life, but the cash value is tied to market performance. There is no downside protection, meaning you can lose money!

As enamored as some are in the financial services world about whole life insurance, I am decidedly not a fan and have not been for decades. It is too inflexible, and the returns are not in the same ballpark as with institutional-grade, flexible premium-type contracts we use for clients (and for myself!) No hate mail, please. Go write your own book if you don't like my opinion. (Said in love … mostly!)

OK … How Does This "Tax-Free" Part Work?

Without getting into the weeds, let me state a critically important IRS guideline. They do not characterize a withdrawal from a life insurance contract as income if it is labeled a "loan." The insurance industry will loan a certain portion of the cash build-up (in excess of the money needed for the contract "reserve"… the money projected to be required to pay the death benefit.) The collateral for the "loan" is the contract cash value. In most cases, the survivor benefit will be reduced by the amount of the outstanding loan(s) upon death.

Am I doing a good enough job explaining this so far? Hang with me a few more paragraphs, and this will all - or mostly - make sense!

Here's the magic … if the money coming out is labeled a loan, there will be no tax on the money received. Just as you are not taxed on the money you borrow to purchase a home, so too the money you receive from the life insurance contract loan is non-taxable.

A big difference, however, is that the loan from the life insurance company does not have to be repaid until or unless death occurs! As explained above, the insurance company reduces the survivor benefit by the outstanding loan amount.

Survivor benefits under IRS Section 101 are not taxable for either income or capital gains taxes. Therefore, the loan "forgiveness" is looked at as being the premature receipt of a tax-free survivor benefit. (Note: Life insurance CAN be subject to federal and state estate/death taxes if not properly structured, so do keep that aspect in mind.)

"But wait," you exclaim breathlessly. (Beginning to sound like a romance novel here ...) "What rate of interest is being charged on the insurance loan, and won't that dramatically impact our net rate of return?"

Well ... what if I told you that the interest rate on these loans is from ... wait for it ... 0% - 0.25% net? What? And, any loan interest due - minimal, if at all - can be paid by the contract.

For now, I am going to leave the curtain closed on the specific mechanics justifying negligible, if any, net interest owed. That is just the way it is ... at least with the newest generation insurance contracts. My own contract has a net borrowing cost of 0% because I have owned the contract for a certain number of years.

And, with these kinds of contracts, the life insurance companies *assume* they are going to be borrowed against and price for it ... as opposed to traditional life insurance contracts. They *don't* want you borrowing against the contracts and charge a 2% - 4% interest rate (and with some companies, reduce your promised dividend rate. The larger the loan outstanding, the greater the reduction in dividends they will pay the insured.)

With the purchase of real estate, there are acquisition costs to be paid to the realtor, escrow, title insurance, etc. So, too, life insurance companies have similar costs. Commissions need to be paid to an advisor, for example, as well as the costs of obtaining underwriting and healthcare information on the insured, a small pro rata charge for company expenses, etc.

These "acquisition costs" are recovered over time ... some stretching out the recovery over 10-15 years, and others right up front. (The latter tends to be those "whole life" companies, which is another reason I am not a fan of these products compared to the newer contract designs.)

The contract loans are calculated based on the net amount available in this after-costs "bucket" and normally allow for borrowing up to 92% of the net values in there.

As you pay premiums into the insurance contract, you build the cash value that the insurance company invests and gives you a portion of the returns.

What do I typically recommend for life insurance contract designs as opposed to the old whole life "dinosaur?" Again, without getting into the weeds, I prefer using something called a "universal life" contract design for my own portfolio as well as for clients.

OK ... for you conspiracy theorists out there, this is not a new world order or religious experience. Universal life is simply the name attached to an insurance design that is "unbundled." That is, the survivor benefit cost is clearly disclosed, as well as internal costs and contract gains. This is as opposed to whole life, which is something I call a "black box." You send in insurance premiums over time, and they do their hocus pocus and credit your contract with some returns over time.

Do watch out for the insurance advisors who tell you your return is 5% or some crazy number that they are crediting to your cash values. In truth, you are only earning that on a portion of the funds … not on the amount you have contributed. (I just ran into another example of this misstatement again today by a "mutual" insurance company that will remain unnamed but whose first initial is "N"! You know who you are!)

Switching gears, in many states, the cash values of a life insurance contract are fully - or at least partially - protected against creditors! Wow. Gotta love that in this litigious society in which we live. Additionally, many states protect the cash values in the event of bankruptcy. (Examples: TX, VA, PA, NY, NV, FL, GA, DE, AZ, and many others.) New Hampshire has zero protection, while several states have unclear protection. Oh well. Some states do not give creditor protection, but do give unlimited protection in the event of bankruptcy. In either case, those protections are quite attractive if you happen to live in one of those states!

So … there are no blanket statements to be made. Understand the laws in your state.

Bottom line ... millions of Americans can have unlimited amounts of assets socked away in life insurance contract(s) and be protected when "life (or death) happens." After all, we are talking about life insurance here!

Random Thought Alert: As Regards the Cost of College These Days

The "investment-grade" life insurance contracts also have properties that often make them a better choice for funding educational expenses than using a Section 529 plan or only using a 529. This assumes you have, ideally, ten years (or more) to fund the insurance contract.

There is a maximum amount of funding per year that can be put into a 529 plan. The life insurance contract, on the other hand, does not have a limit on how much money you can stick away for "future delivery." The only restriction is that you need to purchase a minimum amount of survivor benefit relative to the premiums you are paying each year. (Over time, it lessens.)

Just as a 529 contract allows you to grow money without tax, so too do life insurance contracts. However, the life contract allows you to access money for *any* purpose without tax. On the other hand, 529 allows for tax-favored withdrawals if the money is used for educational purposes *only*. It doesn't have to be an "either-or" decision. You can have both. I have found, however, that clients choose an "overfunded" life insurance contract instead of the 529, assuming we have 10+ years to accumulate funds. The unlimited contributions combined with withdrawal flexibility for any purpose are the two primary benefits clients tell me they value most.

While I am at it, another advantage of owning permanent life insurance - especially the generally faster-accumulating style contracts - is regarding the Federal government form called FAFSA. This stands for the "Free Application for Federal Student Aid" form. While the FAFSA form requires you to list virtually every asset you possess, it does *not* require you to list any life insurance cash values ... even if there are millions of dollars accumulated there!

Private schools do reserve the right to ask about other assets, so understand that life insurance might be an asset you may have to list if your child/children attend a private school ... but not with the FAFSA form (at least in 2026).

How Your Cash Grows Inside the Contract

How Different Permanent Insurance Contracts Grow Their Cash Value

- **Whole Life:** Varies widely according to a formula determined by the insurance company
- **Universal Life:** Growth is tied to either bond portfolio returns *or* an index, like the S&P 500, commonly referred to as an indexed universal life or IUL contract
- **Variable Life:** Cash value invested directly into the market - can either be in a Variable Whole Life or Variable Universal Life form

Having helped clients buy whole life, universal, and variable universal life contracts over my career has given me perspective on the good and bad of each product type. I have owned every type of permanent life insurance listed above at one time or another in my portfolio.

Today, while some will likely disagree, the most flexible design for the greatest number of people is an indexed universal life contract with a top-tier life insurance company. Hence, that is what I have bought for myself and recommend to clients. (See Forbes' list of top life insurance companies for current ratings.)

This is especially true where the end goal is to use the life insurance contract to provide a non-taxable income stream at some point in the future and not have the focus solely on providing the survivor benefit.

Remember waaaaaaaaaaaaay back to the chapter "Taking Inventory - The Map, Compass, and a Pyramid" where we talked about the financial pyramid?

The first layer of the pyramid was building up your emergency and opportunity fund. Part was having cash to cover 3-6 months (or more) of your monthly expenses. The other part was building up cash value in a life insurance contract, again for emergencies and opportunities.

That's what we're doing here. I know life insurance isn't exciting, but trust me that as you continue to deposit money faithfully (we generally recommend 75% going into your cash account and 25% going into your insurance accounts), exercise that discipline, and see those values continue to grow, it gets more exciting. That growing value then allows you more opportunities to invest in alternative tools, giving you additional options to accelerate the growth of your net worth. And that's when it starts to get really exciting!

Remember, gravity is greatest when you're first leaving Mother Earth, but the farther out you get, the faster you can go. This is the same principle, the more money you accumulate (even though it's harder in the early years), to set aside *and keep it set aside* as you develop those discipline muscles, you'll all of a sudden find lots of doors that are opening to accelerate the growth of your net worth.

That 25% Savings Into Insurance

Let's "lean into" the idea of using an "indexed universal life insurance contract" as a way to accumulate funds for present and future delivery.

The name itself? Universal Life Insurance (also called "Adjustable Life Insurance") is so-called because the premiums can be scaled up and down. It allows for unscheduled additions of extra contributions and withdrawals of either a taxable or non-taxable outcome. It is by far the most flexible (adjustable) permanent life insurance contract you will find.

Understand that the IRS provides guidelines on the amount that can be included in a contract, deducted from it, and so forth. Certain actions could jeopardize the non-taxability of income if one were to operate outside the compliance of the IRS guidelines. Ask me to translate that during our 20-minute complimentary conversation if you would like!

Why do they call it "indexed?" If you said, "because it is linked to an equity index of some sort - like the S&P 500 Index - well, aren't you the clever one? You get a gold star! And, most often, it IS the S&P 500 Index that it is aligned with. Granted, it might be a one-year measurement, a two-year measurement, or a five-year (you see where this is going!) measurement. But it could also be an international index or combination, etc.

Universal life contracts, and especially indexed contracts, grow asset values much quicker than whole life contracts. In fact, premiums are roughly 30% - 40% less with a universal life contract than with whole life. Or, you can put in the same amount of premium and have more to show for it over time … usually!

But wait! If this is tied to an equity market index, what if the index goes negative? Do I lose cash values in that situation?

Another of the major attractions of this type of contract is that if the markets take a tumble, there is a downside protection factor built into the contract. If the index is -18.1% (as the S&P 500 Index was in 2022), your contract will credit you with a 0% return.

This illustrates the concept that one of the best ways to grow your money over time is not to LOSE your money in a down cycle. (Or lose very little net of fees ...) That downside protection is an important feature of these types of contracts.

To be fair, however, we have to point out that these products also have (in most cases) a ceiling on the upside potential. (But, my own contract allows for a higher return above the cap if I am willing to pay a little extra premium for that right.)

As well, some contracts (like the one I use for myself) allow a leveraging feature. If my net return was 8% for the year, I might get a 16% return overall using a performance enhancement bonus. (Note: This performance bonus rider can be taken off - put on a little - or a lot from year to year ... and therefore, the fee for this rider can be zero to 7.5% per year.) Since good years come approximately twice as often as bad, over time, the use of performance bonuses can really help increase the ultimate accumulation. (While some might play with the rider turned on or off, I leave mine switched on. After all, 2023 was supposed to be a bad year in the equity markets, and it earned 26.3% net. Pretty impressive "bad" year!)

And, when/if you need some quick cash, a withdrawal request to the insurance company normally just takes a few days, and you have the cash in hand.

For example, I was able to buy a rental home in an upscale community in San Diego for 22 cents on the dollar. I came in with a cash offer ahead of my more affluent neighbors, thanks to my cash value life insurance (and thanks to the money in my "Broom Fund!" See chapter about "Building a Positive Addiction to Savings.")

The above is an illustration of using your cash value for an opportunity. But what about when you're in retirement? Or, perhaps there is a financial emergency?

You might recall in our conversation about the fancy concept titled "Sequence of Returns Risk" that having multiple buckets to draw income from is quite important.

Take a quick minute to look back at the $1.6 million difference chart we showed in the Chapter "Diversifying Income Streams and Sequence of Returns Risk." That chart shows the benefit of allowing your investments a year to "rest" following a negative return year in the equity/bond markets. If, during that rest year, you would instead draw out retirement income from another source, like your life insurance contract, using this approach, it is no exaggeration to say the difference could amount to millions of dollars in your retirement account(s)!

By funding a contract using an IRS "guideline minimum death benefit" to allow for maximum growth, the cash values are built to provide you with a stable bucket to draw from. With its downside protection floor, these contracts are much more predictable in market downturns and recessions to use as a retirement funding source. We can open the "income spigot" up in years when our investment accounts have gone negative and then return to our equities accounts when they're performing positively.

And again, the income received is itself income tax-free when correctly designed, which allows you to take out less from the contract or have more net in your pocket after-tax if you take out an amount equal to your distributions from your taxable retirement accounts.

One more thing: ultimately, there is a tax-free survivor benefit, although we usually squeeze the face amount down to the smallest amount allowed by the IRS. In all but the most unusual cases, there is still more ultimately coming back than we put into the contract, either as income, survivor benefit, or both.

As the pastor said in his sermon, after saying "just one more thing," I have one last point!

Many of the newest life insurance contracts also allow you to tap into the survivor benefit to pay for long-term care needs under certain conditions. This is also tax-free when designed correctly.

OK, one more note of advice. (It REALLY is the last one, I promise.) These types of contracts have many more "moving parts" than a traditional whole life contract. While we have helped hundreds of clients purchase this type of product, there are unquestionably other experienced advisors who could help in this conversation for you.

To start with, make sure your advisor is a Chartered Life Underwriter (CLU). Also, that they have experience in helping clients buy various types of permanent life insurance. (By the way, the CLU is for life insurance as the CPA designation is for accountants, so do be sure to look for it.)

Be aware that some advisors are affiliated with companies that only sell one form of permanent coverage. I am sorry, but no one product is best for every situation … no matter what the agent says!

Ask the advisor how many different types of permanent coverage contracts they have helped consumers buy, which types they used … and specifically, how many indexed universal life (IUL) insurance contracts they have helped to structure. How many different companies and IUL products have they used over the last 24-36 months? (I can tell you that we have used at least four different insurance companies with their own unique products for different client goals, age, health, etc.)

I can say they were all IUL contracts, but as stated above, IUL contracts can be complicated. You do not want to be the insurance advisor's "learning experience." Get it set up correctly and optimally the first time out.

The Most Important Thing

What matters most of all is that you insure your life for an appropriate amount. If you have limited financial resources, getting the survivor benefit is an appropriate option for your needs. If some or all of that can be indexed life insurance, terrific! But probably, there has to be at least some of it that is going to be short-term and then get converted over time.

Some insurance needs are temporary, such as covering a mortgage on a home or property, or a debt. In which case, at the end of a certain number of years, that debt is gone. Well then, buy a life insurance contract to cover that period of 10, 15, or 20 years.

But some needs are ongoing: income replacement for your spouse or your children, money for the family, and estate planning ... those are typically ongoing needs, and therefore, buy a life insurance contract that will be with you for your lifetime.

Action Items

1. Find an insurance agent you trust who has experience with various types of permanent life insurance contracts - preferably with designations to show they have some training!
2. Look at your budget and see how much you can dedicate *today* to funding a contract that makes sense for your budget
3. Get quotes and read the fine print!
4. Apply and lock the contract in place to get the snowball rolling

CHAPTER SUMMARY

Real Estate Income Bucket

I have no ulterior motive in saying this, but I wholeheartedly believe that everyone should own some form of real estate in their portfolio. (Note: Having a home does not count - unless you plan to sell it and live under a rock!) Here's how to get started and a breakdown of what types of real estate investing may work best for your personality.

Major takeaways from this chapter will include:

- Heck, yes, you should invest in real estate!
- Real estate and its correlation with the stock market vs. historical non-correlation
- Recognize that owning real estate comes with, at times, stressful periods
- Real estate comes in active and passive flavors
- Think beyond merely housing - what about self-storage, senior healthcare, RV parks, etc.?
- Challenges to real estate investing
- Real Estate Investment Trusts (REITs) & Crowd-sourcing
- Where could you find the money to invest in real estate?
- Real estate investing using a retirement account - advantages and disadvantages
- Understanding this thing called "depreciation"?

Real Estate Income Bucket

First of all, should you own investment real estate at all?

The short answer is … heck, yes! It's a terrific way to generate inflation-resistant income (assuming that you increase the rents you charge to your tenants!) Many, many Americans have become multi-millionaires by owning real estate.

It's also a great way to suck up a lot of money and get into a very stressful situation or have unexpected negative events occur … just like the rest of life!

We've been "unpacking" various kinds of investments for your retirement portfolio. Generally, the more options … the greater the diversity … the better the outcome(s). Not every type of investment goes up at the same time. Some asset classes, in fact, go down as stocks go up. The opposite is true as well. (This is referred to as a "correlation" or "non-correlation.")

Once upon a time, real estate was considered an "alternative investment" or a – fancy word alert – "non-correlated investment." Huh? This means if something is non-correlated, returns from another asset class do not dictate the return of a second type of asset.

For example, for many years, real estate was considered a non-correlated asset, meaning that when stocks went up, real estate didn't necessarily go up in value as well. Their returns were not tied to each other. At least, that was the consensus thinking of decades prior.

Then came the great recession of 2008, when we discovered that the returns on real estate could be very much tied to stock returns. Both asset classes went down … hard.

The point of this chapter is to inform and educate, but also present the reality that this is just an entry-level conversation. If you want to dig into the subject further, whole courses are taught on real estate investing.

Before we get too far into this chapter, we need to make clear again that ***"past performance is no guarantee of future returns. Investing in real estate involves risk, including the potential loss of principal."*** *While there is a remote chance that you could lose all of your investment, with real estate, anything is possible!*

The simple truth is that today, the returns of investment real estate are much more consistent with the returns of the stock market. When one category rises, the other often follows suit.

There is a "positive correlation." Nothing wrong with that ... it's just that you might have two major asset classes – stocks and real estate – going DOWN at the same time! If you are not prepared, this could be a big financial "ouch"...

Oh, and for those of you reading this book saying to yourself that real estate doesn't go down in value ... well - just you wait! (Where were you in 2008? Or, how about the 1990s?)

Or would you like to hear about the lot I purchased in Costa Rica, assuming I would build a vacation home? I made a nice profit, but when I decided not to build and sell the lot instead, the great recession had kicked in, and I couldn't sell that lot at any price. Not just a lowball offer ... I got NO offers, at least at the time. Eventually, I did get my investment money back, but only after a couple of years of waiting.

Oh, and the fractional interest I had in an apartment building outside Houston? I sold that for 19 cents on the dollar after getting hammered by a hurricane and COVID later on. But it was the brain-eating amoeba discovered in the nearby recreational lake that really did me in! Oh my ... I'm still in therapy over that one! (Not really ... but I could be! That was a tough one ...)

So ... don't tell me that real estate cannot go down in value ... because it totally can.

But real estate, like any investment, has a cycle. From high to low to high again, the typical investment cycle is 3-7 years. (Well, not sure about crypto, but OK).

Now that you have run for the exits on the idea of having real estate ownership in your portfolio ... come back! It is a terrific investment, and everyone needs to have some form of investment real estate in their portfolios. This is true whether you look great wearing a tool belt or don't know the top from the bottom of a hammer.

Flavors of Real Estate Investing

Rental income from real estate comes in two "flavors." There's active (although I'm not sure I want to know what active flavor tastes like), where we invest in a piece of land or building and then either act as the property manager or hire an outside manager.

Then there's the "passive" flavor. In this one, you invest funds into some type of real estate investment, but have no management responsibility. The real estate syndicator or sponsor does all of the "heavy lifting" – buying, selling, developing, building, management, etc. Then, you get a share of any income generated and typically a share in any profits coming upon the sale of the (hopefully) appreciated property/building, land, and so forth.

Let's start with active.

If you're handy, consider buying a home/duplex/condo, fixing it up, and then renting it out for income. Over time, as your tenants pay rent, good things will usually happen … like having someone else pay down your mortgage!

By the way, this assumes COVID 2 doesn't strike and the government doesn't tell your tenants they don't have to honor their rent commitment, but you still owe the bank your mortgage payments. Another very good reason for eventually having 24 months of expenses covered in your "Broom Fund" once you get into real estate.

Your mortgage goes down, and your tenant is paying for it. Plus, you make some extra cash on the side. Sweet! The longer you keep it, the more rent you can charge, the more debt gets paid off, and the more equity you gain!

Then, you can borrow against the equity in that rental asset, in most cases, buy another income property, and repeat the process all over again!

Many Americans have become millionaires doing the above … one property at a time, and then two at a time, etc.

We once had a client who bought small fixer-uppers after she was forced to retire because of arthritis from the school at which she worked. One small house fixed up and rented out after another … and eventually, she was worth well over ten million dollars. And this was in the early 2000s, so that estate would be worth a significantly greater amount today.

How do they do that?

Probably by starting simple. It may look like:

- Buying a property
- Fixing it up

- Selling it
- Buying another one

Or it may look like:

- Buy a property
- Fix it up
- Rent it out
- Refinance the mortgage to take equity out
- Go buy another one with the cash from the first rental asset

Then, you may eventually go into buying a multi-unit property - duplex, triplex, apartment building, etc. More income opportunities. More opportunities for tenants to say their dog ate their rent check!

This flavor is for the person who can and wants to be actively involved. If they're clever, they can do it that way. Not only is there income to be made, but a unique feature we'll describe in a moment, called "depreciation," allows a certain amount of income not to be taxable at all! What a concept!

So, whether it is buying and fixing up a single-family residence or a multi-unit apartment building, if you are clever at fixing things or have connections and can get the work done inexpensively, being an "active real estate investor" might be just the thing for you. Way to go!

After we finish our high-fiving and doing a happy dance, the very next thing to do is to begin boosting your "broom account" to 12 to 24 months of cash to cover expenses. You will want to have extra money set aside so that if you have trouble finding a quality tenant, or your roof springs a leak, or the water heater goes out … you don't get into trouble.

Remember, Murphy's Law states that "whatever can go wrong … WILL go wrong." (And, O'Toole's Corollary, that "Bread always falls jam side down!")

You can make a great deal of money over time with investment real estate … but you can also spend a great deal of money at times *before* you start receiving anything! In case you haven't looked into it recently … a new roof is usually expensive!

That Sounds Difficult … What's the Passive Method?

So … that is what "active" investing looks like today. What about "passive" investing?

Are you like me? Do you create a community hazard by attempting any "fix-it" project? (I did manage to replace my windshield wipers on the same day I started the project. Hurray for me!) If so, you might be better off investing in real estate programs through a syndicator or sponsor.

Recently, I invested in two institutional real estate funds focused on building apartments in Texas, Florida, and the mid-Atlantic (North and South Carolina primarily). They are 3-4 year programs after which the managers will sell the apartment complexes for a profit (hopefully) by:

1. Fixing up the properties
2. Raising rents
3. Attracting better quality tenants
4. Eventually selling to a new buyer

The value of a building is in the rent being paid. The higher the total amount of rental income and the number of long-term renters, the more this translates into a higher sales price.

While you may make more of a return if you control the variables yourself, there is a risk of becoming stretched too thin. Things happen that are out of your control sometimes. Borrowing rates increase. City/State/Federal governments can impose new regulations … such as the COVID restrictions.

On the other hand, if you invest with an institutional sponsor or syndicator, you are normally classified as a "limited partner" and protected from liability if things blow up. You can only lose what you've invested in the project.

No one wants to lose money, of course, but if you borrow $500,000 or $1,000,000 to buy a property, things don't work out, and now have the bank coming after you … well, I predict sleepless nights in your future. The banks usually require collateral for the loan that is much more than just the down payment on the property.

On the passive side, the limited partnership investment can be as little as $25,000 - $50,000 … a much smaller amount of money to risk losing. (In many of these investments, though, you must be an "accredited investor" … a concept we unpack two chapters further down!)

Active is much more risky, but can provide much greater rewards. That's the good news.

The bad news is that "life happens." I have had so many unexpected things happen in my real estate holdings. Fortunately, I've dodged the bullet on a lot of things … brain-eating amoebas are hard to predict, dodge, or even think about for too long. Keeping nice big stacks of cash down at the credit union and in life insurance contracts, however, has "de-risked" all but the greatest potential liabilities.

Active or passive, it is a great idea to diversify your portfolio (and your returns) by investing in income-producing real estate such as apartments, self-storage, senior healthcare, and even … wait for it … Recreational Vehicle (RV) parks!

Yes … you heard me right. We have a new prospective client generating millions of dollars through buying, fixing up, and creating whole communities for those spending several hundred thousand dollars on a "camping site" for their $1.5 - $2.5 million RV.

How Much Money Do You Need to "Get Into Real Estate"?

Before investing in income-producing real estate, it's essential to do your homework. Sit down (or find) a professional investment advisor who can help sort out what it is you're looking for - and how much money you should consider investing.

Some of the institutional projects we work with require as little as $25,000 to put down on their investments. Most require at least $50,000 or more. And you typically don't borrow money to invest in these projects if it's a passive investment.

On the active side, you will need the down payment for the property, plus cash to fix it. I have discovered the hard way that sometimes the "fix-up costs" are the most expensive parts of the purchase!

One drawback to real estate investing is coming up with the money to invest! Buying stocks/bonds/mutual funds/ETFs can be done over time and in smaller amounts. Investing in real estate usually requires larger amounts of cash in one chunk.

Further, that money to invest comes after paying taxes - at least when starting out. As said, over time, you can take a non-taxable loan against a property with equity and buy another asset that way ... but generally not at the start of assembling your real estate building empire!

REITs Are a Wonderful "Low Barrier to Entry"

Good news! There's a lower-cost point of entry, with some offerings starting as low as investments of just $1,000. It's called Real Estate Investment Trusts or REITs.

REITs can be traded like stocks or ETFs. When you buy a share, you begin receiving dividends from the property's rental income. This is taxed as regular income, and REIT companies must distribute at least 90% of their rental income as dividends to shareholders to avoid being taxed themselves. (Good to know they aren't holding out on you!)

It can create a steady stream of income, and they can also be liquid – a rarity in real estate – since you can buy and sell some REITs on most exchanges.

A more recent arrival on the stage for anyone wishing to invest in real estate and also open to non-accredited investors is crowdsourcing. Several new offerings are springing up to allow individuals to invest very small amounts of money into almost any type of real estate you can imagine. Clever idea!

Crowdsourcing is a way for an investor to borrow money, but instead of using a traditional lending institution, they'll borrow smaller amounts from hundreds or thousands of people. But, like any investment, make sure you vet these people and companies properly!

REITs and crowdsourcing are enabling a new type of real estate investor to build a portfolio. But how do you come up with the sometimes sizeable amount of money required initially to start investing in larger transactions?

OK...Where Can I Get Money to Start?

This is my favorite part. Ready?

You get the money (or at least some) from your other buckets!

Remember, in the last chapter, we talked about owning a cash-value life insurance contract to create a source of tax-free money for whatever you want? Many people use that as leverage to jump on amazing real estate opportunities when they appear. (I was able to buy a property for 29 cents on the dollar thanks to savings and the cash values in my life insurance contract!)

The more buckets you have, the easier it is to acquire new ones. This is why building that positive addiction to saving is such an important first step!

What else could you do?

What about tapping into money that's accumulated in your 401(k) retirement account?

Assuming your plan allows for participant loans, the law permits each person the ability to borrow up to $50,000 from their retirement account! If you are married, there is another potential $50,000. (We go into this in greater detail in our chapter called "401(k) Bucket.")

There is also something called a "self-directed IRA," for example, which can allow you to invest in real estate. (This could be either using a pre-tax IRA or a Roth IRA.) I invested in an LLC through my self-directed IRA, which in turn invested on a fractional basis into that ill-fated apartment building with the brain-eating amoeba in the lake.

Bear in mind, if you do use your retirement accounts … it's not the perfect solution. Yes, it is often the only place where an investor might have a big wad of cash for investing in real estate.

On the other hand, some of the advantages of real estate investing are lost when investing through a retirement account. Such things as:

- Using depreciation to offset income
- Long-term capital gains treatment upon sale of the investment vs. treating the income as taxable ordinary income once you take retirement
- Mortgage interest deductions
- Property tax deductions
- Buying a property and renting some (or all) of it to yourself

As said above, one of the biggest disadvantages of buying real estate through a tax-deferred retirement account is the inability to shelter income by using something called depreciation.

You Keep Mentioning Depreciation. What Is It?

Depreciation is theoretically the wearing out of a property. The longer you own a piece of property, the less it is worth because the building is getting older. It needs repairs that will cost you money. Hence, the idea of depreciation.

The government gives you the ability to write off depreciation against your income. It can be used to offset some of the income that you receive from your real estate investment because of a pre-supposed decrease in value. (Whether that actually happens or not.)

The bottom line is that if you're handy with your hands and want more risk, take the active path. Buy a house, fix it, and rent it out.

If you want the lower-risk option (or aren't interested in unclogging someone else's shower!), the passive approach may suit you better. Invest in real estate through professional (aka institutional) real estate syndications.

So whichever type of real estate works best for your handiness or risk tolerance, get some real estate in your portfolio!

Action Items

1. Decide which "flavor" of real estate investor better fits you
2. If you're in a position to buy real estate, start on the path of the appropriate flavor for you
3. If you are not yet in a position to buy real estate, start accumulating some REITs to diversify your portfolio

CHAPTER SUMMARY

Buckets for Self–Employed People

If you skipped the 401(k) chapter because you work for yourself, we've got you covered here! In this chapter, we cover some unique buckets that people who work for themselves can take advantage of, too!

Major takeaways from this chapter will include:

- IRA options
- Contribution limits
- Roth IRAs vs. traditional IRAs
- Putting yourself on a salary
- Positive addiction to saving via automation and direct deposit keeps you on budget
- What in the world is a "Solo K"?

Buckets for Self-Employed People

There's a lot of noise on the internet about various kinds of retirement plans. But, if you're self-employed, what's the "right" kind of retirement plan for you to set up for yourself, and why?

Before we get super specific … let's take a quick minute to understand what some states have enacted for retirement programs. The State of California, for example, as of 1/1/2023, requires employers with five or more employees to provide a retirement plan. Or, employers must facilitate allowing employees to contribute to the State-run retirement plan. This includes all employees working over 20 hours a week or 1,000 hours a year.

Five more states (Massachusetts, Connecticut, Illinois, Oregon, and Washington) have the auto-enroll IRA mandate. Five more, as of today, have it in the works (Colorado, Maine, New Jersey, New York, and Maryland).

Although there is no mandatory contribution required of employers yet, give it a few more years! It will no doubt be there!

The Solo K

Too often, self-employed individuals are told to set up an IRA or a SEP (Self-Employed Pension) when they should be setting up a "Solo K" plan instead. I love CPAs ... we receive many referrals from them. Unfortunately, in this area, my experience is that they don't typically suggest their clients set up a Solo K. Most often, they tell them to set up a SEP.

Well, in a SEP, the amount you can put into it is a percentage of your income. The SEP allows 20% of your income before tax, but after expenses. (Technically, the limit is 25%, but if you do 20% of the net, it works out with 25%.) For example, if someone has $100,000 income after tax and they put away 20% or $20,000, that is 25% of $80,000.

A Solo 401(k) allows you to set money aside on a dollar-for-dollar basis, just like an IRA/Roth IRA, except with higher limits. You can contribute the first $24,500 of income earned in 2026 or $32,500 if you are age 50 or older and qualify for the additional $8,000/year "catch-up provision." Your business can also add additional funds as a percentage of your overall income on top of your contributions.

Without diving too far into the formulas (talk with your accountant about that), let's say you have $100,000 of total income. That will turn into roughly $94,000 after business expenses like rent, phones, parking, etc. You could put away $32,500 (assuming you're 50 or older) plus 20% of the original $94,000 – another $18,800. Giving you a total contribution for the year of $51,300.

In short, a Solo K allows you to put more money away than a SEP plan using the same amount of income. (There are some exceptions if your income is significantly higher, but you get the drift … right?)

And, wait, it gets even better ...

If you own your own business and your spouse does as well, you can each set up your own 401(k) but only have to file one 5500! (Oh, and the 5500 is a reporting document for retirement accounts. It's not terribly sexy, but it's a very important form to get filed every year!)

Admittedly, with all the formulas and such, this is not something to try at home. Probably best to have a quick conversation about your goals - taxable income - and your "Five Hows." We can talk through which type of retirement plan would be best for you as an entrepreneur now and for the future.

The Most Common Advice on the Internet

So, what do you do if you followed your CPA's advice and already have an IRA? How does that work?

If you have *any earned income*, you can contribute to a traditional individual retirement account (IRA) and receive a tax deduction for the contribution. Alternatively, you may wish to fund what's called a Roth IRA rather than a traditional IRA, but more on that in a minute.

A traditional IRA or Roth IRA has a contribution limit of $7,500 in 2026. If you're age 50 or older, you get an additional $1,100 to set aside - a "catch-up contribution." So, if you are age 50 and older, you can put away a total of $8,600 each year, and it is tax-deductible if the contribution is going into a traditional IRA.

One other quick point about Roth IRAs.

There is a 5-year "seasoning" (or to age 59 ½, whichever is longer) requirement for funding the account before you can take withdrawals. You *can* access the funds prior, but the gains become taxable … which sorta defeats the point of having the Roth to start with!

So, because of the requirement above, open an account as soon as you can, regardless of the amount of money you are contributing. Get the five-year meter running (or to age 59 ½.).

If your current income is too high to set up a Roth (anything above $252,000 joint taxable income in 2026 makes you ineligible), consider converting a portion of an existing IRA to become a Roth IRA. Bear in mind that the amount of money coming out of your traditional IRA into your Roth will be currently taxable! So, keep it small in most cases ... just enough to fund the Roth IRA and start creating your tax-free account. You can add more to it later ... (or you can always add more to *mine* later, too!)

As noted, a Roth IRA has the same contribution limits and, just like a traditional IRA, grows with no tax. *Unlike* a traditional IRA, however, you receive no deduction for your contribution. So why do it?

With a Roth, while there is no deduction up front, all the money is tax-free while it is growing AND when it comes out.

And two more benefits of using a Roth IRA! There are no required minimum distributions from a Roth, in contrast to a traditional IRA and 401(k), which require distributions beginning at age 73. Also, Roth IRA distributions do not potentially increase the cost of Medicare premiums as could the taxable distributions of traditional IRAs and 401(k) or other retirement programs.

Bear in mind that both traditional and Roth IRAs have earned income limits that will not allow you to set up or continue funding an existing plan ($168,000 for singles, $252,000 filing jointly for 2026).

Several factors go into choosing whether a traditional or Roth IRA (or Roth 401(k)) makes sense for your situation. So, again, let's have a quick chat and evaluate which would be better for you.

Put Yourself on a Salary If You Aren't Already

I do recommend setting money aside on a regular, automated basis. I transfer $X,XXX twice a month automatically to my savings account at the credit union. And remember the concept of "positive addiction"... that what matters more is the habit of saving money ... not how much you are saving ... at least to start. The more you save, typically, the easier it will be to save and the greater the amount of money that you *want* to save. (This also assumes you do not have a spouse who then spends money as soon as they see money in savings! But that is a chapter in a different book!)

I also personally use direct deposit for my paychecks through the business, which is another recommendation. Even though you may be self-employed, put yourself on a salary. Whether you are a salesperson, real estate advisor, investment specialist, or so forth, get off the "feast or famine" roller coaster of unpredictable income. Instead, give yourself a reliable income stream to plan around. It is one of the best things I did on someone's advice decades ago.

The logic is ... great months come, and there's a whole bunch of money. Terrific! The natural tendency, though, is to blow it all. But then comes the month - or months - where nothing comes in or only a little.

Having a set salary allows you to budget around expenses. Anything extra above the amount needed for payroll stays in the company account, and I stay on my regular, twice-a-month paycheck. Doing it this way lets me be more predictive about my expenses and avoid overspending.

I cannot tell you how many times I have appreciated that great counsel.

And, if you find that there is money left over even after setting money aside for savings, retirement plan funding, donations, and everything else, THEN maybe it's time to give yourself a quarterly bonus! Hurray!!

Action Items

1. If you are not on a fixed salary, talk with your CPA about how to do this. You will be very glad you did!
2. Do you have a retirement account? If not (or even if you do), consider using a Solo K. Have your accountant run some "what ifs" and compare it to a SEP or other type of retirement account.

CHAPTER SUMMARY

Investment Buckets for "Accredited Investors"

Once you reach a certain level of wealth, you get access to higher-risk, higher-reward investment opportunities. If you aren't there yet, use these as an extra motivational boost to keep building that addiction to saving. If you are there, have you considered these strategies yet?

Major takeaways from this chapter will include:

- "Accredited investor" - what that means and who qualifies
- Additional investment opportunities that come from qualifying as an accredited investor
- Delaware Statutory Trusts and Private Placements
- Other potential investment options available to accredited investors

Investment Buckets for "Accredited Investors"

"Accredited Investor"... there's a fancy term. What does it mean - who qualifies - and why should you care? Chances are, if you are one, you know what it means. But if you don't, a quick overview is ...

The Securities and Exchange Commission (SEC) allows accredited investors to buy "riskier" or more complex investments not available to the general public. The SEC thinks that investors with a certain net worth are more aware of and educated about potential investment risks. The accredited investor will have the financial experience to understand investments that have more moving parts. An accredited investor will also likely have a financial cushion to absorb any losses if things don't work out in the investment.

You won't get a plaque or a fancy star on your driver's license ... so I hope that is not too disappointing. And the "accredited investor police" will not come knocking for you to prove you meet the qualifications below. (That we have *heard* of anyway!)

The financial sponsors offering these investments are required to ask if you qualify as an accredited investor, but it is ultimately up to the personal integrity of the investor to state whether they qualify or not.

So, what are the qualifications?

1. $1,000,000 of net worth, not counting the equity in your home, *or...*
2. $200,000 annual income each of the last two years and in the current year, if single, *or...*
3. $300,000 annual income each of the last two years and in the current year, joint with a spouse, *or...*
4. Certain careers or designations from the financial services industry also qualify one as an accredited investor, regardless of income or net worth

As you grow your retirement account, those assets also count toward the calculation of your net worth. So, even if you haven't filled your other buckets as much as you would like, many people qualify as accredited investors based on their retirement account values alone, particularly as they approach their target retirement age.

OK ... but so what, R. J.?

"So what" means that as an accredited investor, you have more diversified investment opportunities that potentially can provide higher rates of return over time. What are some examples?

Well, let's roll down through a few:

- Real estate syndication investments
- Hedge funds
- Venture capital
- Private placements
- Farmland
- Fractional interests in life insurance contracts on the lives of others
- Private equity
- Equity crowdfunding

Real estate syndicate offerings (as discussed in the "Real Estate Income Bucket" chapter) can provide a tax-favored income stream prior to or during your retirement years. At the same time, they can help build your net worth, too, through appreciation in the underlying value of the real estate in the investment offering. (This often occurs, but not always!) For the most part, however, these investments require you to be an accredited investor to participate.

Investing in real estate has been good for me overall, but I also have three personal experiences where I got clobbered. In one, I sold for 19 cents on my investment dollar. (Have I mentioned the brain-eating amoebas found in a lake near the apartment building?)

The other two investments allowed me to come out with my original investment money back or a small profit ... but not what I was expecting. Nothing to "write home about." Nonetheless, anytime one invests in real estate, it's best to remember Will Rogers's phrase, "I am not as concerned about the return ON my money ... as the return OF my money!" I agree!

I have invested personally in some other opportunities for accredited investors listed above. Some have done well enough. My early investment in electric cars in 1995, however, was a total flop. So, let's dig into those areas where I have great personal experience and have seen handsome rewards (overall) for myself and our clients.

Let's Start Out by Discussing Delaware Statutory Trusts - Passive Income, Anyone?

Overall, the best outcomes I have seen for diversifying your assets and gaining excellent long-term returns come through either private placements or DSTs, short for Delaware Statutory Trusts. And, no ... you don't have to live in Delaware to own one!

The distinctions between private placements vs. DSTs come down to this:

- Private placements are not permitted for 1031 tax-free exchanges because they may sell or purchase various assets over the time period for which the money is invested

- DSTs *do* qualify as a replacement asset for 1031 exchanges because the assets in the DST are known to investors at the time of sale. The DST sponsor cannot add or remove assets after the DST is made available for investment

DSTs most commonly invest in real estate, as we will describe below, but there are other examples of using healthcare.

The most attractive quality of DST is that it qualifies for a 1031 exchange. Investing in healthcare DST, while it may make great sense from an investment turnaround standpoint, doesn't qualify for a 1031 exchange. So that's why I think real estate is the predominant choice for a Delaware Statutory Trust.

Here's how it works.

Instead of directly investing in a rental income property, for example, you can put your money into a trust managed by a real estate syndication firm. The firm gives you a return and part of the profits while they manage, upgrade, and eventually sell the asset(s). (Some sponsors even build the project from scratch to enhance the returns, but also for some very clever tax planning!)

Having an institutional management team takes away much of the frustration of having rental property … calls at 3 am about broken heating/AC, leaky water heaters, roof repairs, sagging parking lots … the list is quite long!

With most DSTs, there is a profit-sharing allowance in the net profits coming from the sale of the asset. That is, when the real estate is sold (usually 3 - 7 years down the road), you get:

- The return of your initial investment
- Your prorated share of the net profit after selling expenses and the paying off of debt (if any is used in the DST)
- A "preferred return" of some amount

The preferred return - often called "pref" - is a return that the syndication sponsor must pay to investors (after the return of principal) before any profits are available for the sponsor to share.

Now, the preferred return (and even the principal) is not guaranteed. That's why it's so important to find a proven sponsor where this is not their first rodeo. Look for a proven track record of performance across various markets, including the 90s, the 00s, and the 10s. Each of those decades has its own set of woes and worries, as well as wins.

Given the vagaries of real estate, no one can promise that what they have is a preferred return. It just says that if you don't get your principal (bucket #1 money), your pro rata share of the profits (bucket #2), and your preferred return (bucket #3) filled to the levels that were promised, then the sponsor gets zero.

So they have tremendous incentive to ensure that we investors get all three of our buckets filled, or else they don't get their bucket filled!

Some of the most successful areas of real estate investment we're seeing great returns in right now are:

- Housing for "successful seniors"
    - Private pay customers - not low-income or subsidized housing
    - Part of the 11,400 Americans turning 65 every day in 2025!
- Self-storage (we Americans do love our "stuff" combined with dislocation hurdles like death, disability, divorce, health challenges for self or loved ones, etc.)
- Apartments (with higher interest costs, many younger home seekers need to rent rather than purchase)
- High-end recreation vehicle resorts (there are great mental pictures of the guy with sagging jeans and ample stomach, but that is definitely NOT what we're talking about here! Think "Jimmy Buffett Margaritaville.")
- Mobile home parks (with rising housing costs, they are becoming more popular than ever, both as a housing option and as an investment opportunity. People pay their rent above everything else)
- Mixed-use communities, so-called "live-work-play" urban campus (condos, grocery, retail, restaurants)

In addition to the benefits of asset appreciation, much of the income from these projects (especially in the early years) is tax-sheltered from both federal and state income tax. We're currently seeing cash-on-cash returns in the low 5% - 8% range. And, as said above, in addition to the return of the original investment, there is generally a sharing of profits from the sale of the holdings. This can juice the overall returns to 12% - 18% per year! I have even seen some DSTs with investment returns even higher to investors.

Personally, if I can get a net investment return in the 10-15% range per year, with some of that being non-taxable, I am a very happy camper! Especially where I am only required to tie up my capital for 3-4 years in the projects we recommend (and invest in ourselves). And, for those in high-taxed states such as California, New Jersey, Hawaii, Oregon, and Minnesota, a 6% double tax-free income is equivalent to a 10% return pre-tax, assuming a 40% combined tax rate.

My compliance attorney, once again, wants me to make clear that ***"past performance is no guarantee of future returns."*** *Investing in a DST involves risk, including the potential loss of principal. While there is a remote chance that you could lose all of your investment, with real estate, especially, anything is possible!*

Some of these are cash-only types of investments that use no leverage/bank borrowing to purchase the assets. Typically, private placements and Delaware Statutory Trusts (DSTs) will set you back $50,000 - $100,000 minimum investment.

Some of the sponsors are using leverage to increase returns through using OPM … "other people's money" to invest. Even though borrowing rates have risen (2023 & 2024), by keeping the projects only 3 - 5 years in length, the extra cost of debt to be serviced is generally not decreasing, but instead increasing the overall returns projected.

The most popular projects I am finding in this space are far shorter than in the past. Previously (and still with some today), it was common to find the project term to be 10 years.

Now, however, we are finding many sponsors willing to use much shorter time frames before the liquidity event. And, while there is some amount of flexibility for the seller, with debt being 5 years at the longest, the holding period is almost for sure going to be less than the underlying debt.

Here's an Idea That I Predict Nobody Has Told You About!

Remember way back when we were discussing how IRAs are a wrapper around assets? You can put just about whatever you wish into an IRA. Super. Retirement planning 101.

OK … let's move this up a notch.

How about if we purchase a real estate investment in our IRA using our friend, the Delaware Statutory Trust (DST) structure? So far, so good! Right?

Next, and here's where things start to look different … almost exciting! That is, if you think tax reduction, deferral, and elimination strategy is exciting. (Which I DO!)

In most DSTs, the sponsor buys an existing structure - cleans 'em up - and increases the value of the asset to attract a higher-class tenant willing to pay more to receive that value. All good …

But, there are some DST sponsors that will occasionally build their own building/project from the ground up. One of my favorite sponsors does this in housing for successful seniors. They build a beautiful facility with state-of-the-art healthcare, entertainment, chefs, furnishings/decor, and so forth.

There will be a step-up in value once the project is finished with construction, and happy new residents are in and paying a premium for the best-of-the-best. Prior to accepting tenants, however, and starting the cash flow for the project, a valuation is done on the project. Perhaps not surprisingly, there is a reduction in the value of the asset because there isn't income yet, and they've expensed millions of dollars to build the project. The value of the asset is, on average, 35% less than where things began!

It's at this point that a Roth conversion is done with that part of the IRA invested in the real estate program. Sure, you'll pay taxes on that part being rolled over from the IRA to a Roth IRA in that year. But then you will recover the, on average, 35% reduction in the value of your principal, plus receive income for each year invested.

The project in mind has a "pref rate" of 12% per year. This means that unless the investor receives 12% per year once the project sells, the sponsor doesn't receive anything from the profits coming from the sale. That's an incentive!

So, as a recap, the investor:

- Receives a 35% reduction (on average) in the amount reportable at the time of IRA to Roth IRA conversion
- Pays less tax on the reportable income at conversion as a result
- Pays zero taxes on all future gains and income because of the Roth IRA rules

Woah, OK. That got technical fast. Let's look at an easy math example.

Jane has $100,000 in her IRA. (She is, of course, an accredited investor.) She invests in this special breed of DST.

The project takes three years to build. Her $100,000 investment is now officially valued at $65,000. Jane converts it to a Roth IRA. She reports and pays tax on the $65,000. Then, BOOM, the liquidity event happens several years later. Assuming the project eventually sells for a profit, the initial investment value is restored. So, she has $100,000 plus 12% for every year between her initial investment and the sales event. Let's call it four years. (It's been three on the previous projects.)

Jane now has $148,000 in a Roth IRA that will continue to grow and eventually distribute tax-free!

Not All Real Estate Tax-Free (1031) Exchanges Are Created Equal

Now, here's another important aspect of DSTs.

Often I will hear, "R. J., I want/need to do a 1031 exchange because otherwise I will be killed with taxes. But, what if I can't find a replacement property in the absurdly short time limit allowed? I will still end up paying a boatload of taxes!"

Great news! You can use a DST for all or part of a 1031 exchange.

In a 1031 exchange, you have six weeks to identify potential replacement properties for the asset(s) being sold. You may have your eyes already on a replacement real estate asset, but what if that replacement asset is not equal to or greater in value than the asset(s) being sold?

Here's a solution ... name one or two different DST program offerings to your list of identified replacement properties. In so doing, naming this alternative investment class helps ensure you have more options available to invest your sale proceeds. A 1031 exchange is hard enough without worrying about having something(s) to exchange into and the stressful negotiations that frequently come.

Using the above approach is why I call this planning strategy the "1031 E-Z" method of selling. It greatly reduces the anxiety frequently associated with 1031s, as well as providing an income without management. Often, this is referred to as "mailbox money," where you watch the monthly income drop into your checking account or show up in your mailbox ... without you having to return a single call to a tenant or tent the place for termites!

Even if you don't qualify *yet*, keep saving and working on your other buckets, and one day - hopefully soon - you'll be adding DSTs and private placements into your own investment portfolio!

Action Items

1. If you qualify, give yourself a gold star and consider where DSTs/private placement may make sense to add to your portfolio
2. If you aren't an accredited investor quite yet, perhaps make a list of ways you can accelerate your asset growth to reach that benchmark!

SECTION 5

How Come?

CHAPTER SUMMARY

Life on Purpose and Increasing Your Longevity!

I've known too many people who retired with no plan on how to spend their time. "Doing nothing" gets old quickly, trust me.

With that in mind, let's tackle the last of the Five How Questions, "How come?" How will your life leave a lasting, positive impact on the lives of others and/or your community?

Major takeaways from this chapter will include:

- Identify meaningful goals for the retirement stage of life and live longer!
- "Trial run" retirement to see what life will look like and what changes you would potentially implement to improve the quality of living
- Research on retiring later and living longer
- The importance of planning ahead to ensure that your days have meaning instead of simply waiting to die

Life on Purpose and Increasing Your Longevity!

Part of our client questionnaire includes a "Life on Purpose" list. We ask the following:

- **What do you love doing?** What do you want to do more of?
- **What do you hate doing?** What do you want to do less of?
- When you look back over your life, **what brought you the greatest satisfaction and joy?**
- As you look ahead, **what's on your "bucket list?"**

We've found that people, even the financially very successful ones, very often have not taken the time to sit down and determine what is really meaningful in their lives.

Then, research shows that when people enter retirement, they need to start over, figuring out what makes their life meaningful.

(There is a wonderful TEDx talk by Dr. Riley Moynes called "The 4 Phases of Retirement" if you're interested.)

Recently, at my men's Bible study, one in our group shared that he was planning to retire this year and was feeling somewhat anxious. When I probed a little more about that anxiety, he responded that he did not know what he would be doing in retirement. He has no hobbies to speak of and is staring at a blank sheet. Given that this was his second retirement, I was especially intrigued.

At his age of 70 and looking to be in excellent health, I shared with him the research that shows he will have a shorter life expectancy … *unless* he identifies meaningful life goals for this next stage of his life.

Next, I shared with him the story of a friend of ours who retired from a comfortable government job. One of the perks was early retirement, and he went for it.

Interestingly, however, it wasn't long before he ended up returning to his old position, albeit only two days a week. "There are only so many movies to see alone during the day in an empty theater," he said. "That got old fast."

My point to my friend considering retirement is that, for many, careers provide structure to our lives five days a week (or more). And the weekends focus on chores and rest. Then, the cycle starts all over again Monday morning. It's a nice rhythm that seems to "work" for many!

But when we interrupt that cycle, it leaves many feeling depressed, lonely, anxious, and purposeless. It is like a "COVID lockdown," but for the rest of our lives! (I don't know about you, but I was feeling quite depressed for a time, being at home all day and not having regular interaction with others.) For many, COVID greatly limited our activities, which would normally invigorate us and keep us socially engaged … especially if our friends are still working their "9-5s."

Once you leave your job for good, there's suddenly a lot of time to fill. Have you truly thought through how you will use it in retirement? Or, as one spouse said to a friend of mine who retired early, "I married you for dinner. I didn't marry you for lunch." She was, of course, *mostly* kidding, but he was still smart enough to get the hint and find some other ways to be productively active during the day.

One idea I've found myself recommending is a "trial run" retirement to get a glimpse of what your life will be like once you punch the eject button and your wonderful spouse and/or colleagues throw you a party.

A Retirement "Test Drive"

Take a bunch of time off from work, 1-2 months if possible… but if you can only get 2 weeks, that's a good start. But instead of planning the family vacation with every minute detailed out in a spreadsheet, test run your "what on earth am I going to do with all this time?" retirement plan.

Being a couch potato or spending every afternoon at the driving range may sound nice in the middle of a stressful week ... but in practice? My bet is you'll get really, really bored…and/or drive your spouse nuts … or both.

Study after study has shown that people who retire early tend to die sooner, and that includes a recent study from Oregon State University.

To start with, doesn't it make sense that people near retirement age who have existing health issues would be among the first to jump the job ship? After all, they don't feel well, work is a stressor, and if their illness is serious, they want to spend whatever time they have left with family and friends.

Getting medical treatments can also be a black hole, so chances are there is added stress even when your boss *isn't* being a shmuck. So what do these people do? They retire early, that's what! And then, because they were sick, they died. But doesn't logic tell us that it was their illness, not their retirement, that was the cause of their death? Can early retirement really be a risk factor for early death?

The OSU study tried to address that question head-on. The researchers found that healthy adults who retired one year past age 65 had an 11 percent lower risk of death from all causes, even when taking into account demographic, lifestyle, and health issues. Even people who described themselves as unhealthy lived longer if they kept working.

"It may not apply to everybody, but we think work brings people a lot of economic and social benefits that could impact the length of their lives," said Chenkai Wu, the lead author of the study.

The findings have been published in the Journal of Epidemiology and Community Health. The research team reviewed data collected from 1992 through 2010 via the Healthy Retirement Study, funded by the National Institute on Aging.

Since poor health is a reason people retire early and can also lead to earlier death, the researchers aimed to mitigate its impact. They divided the group into two categories: unhealthy retirees, who indicated that health was a factor in their decision to retire, and healthy retirees, who indicated that health was not a factor.

Now, stay with me here … during the study period, about 12 percent of the healthy and 26 percent of the unhealthy retirees died. Healthy retirees who worked a year longer had an 11 percent lower risk of mortality, while unhealthy retirees who worked a year longer had a 9 percent lower mortality risk.

Working a year longer had a positive impact on the study participants' mortality rate, regardless of their health status. Obviously, there are many factors to consider, but the bottom line is that the findings seem to indicate that people who remain active and engaged draw a benefit with improved longevity.

On to The Planning!

It's critical to plan your free time in retirement as thoroughly as you plan your finances or a vacation.

How many of us would take a two-week trip to Europe without spending time in advance to consider:

- How we'll get there
- Where we'll stay
- What we will see when we get there
- How we are getting home and when

How many have spent at least as much time considering how they will spend their next 20 – 40 years? Remember, a 70-year-old today is projected to have another 27.4 years to the halfway point, where half of those 70-year-olds are dead, but half are still alive.

Your money needs to survive that long, but so does your purpose for living!

How many of us have heard the maxim, "If you fail to plan, you are planning to fail?" Which, in this case, could be applied to, "If you fail to plan for how you will spend the rest of your life, you are planning to fail on finding a meaningful reason to get out of bed each morning!"

Sketching out even a rough list of ways to be socially and physically active counts as planning. It helps prevent the real probability of dying too soon or having significant health challenges that may not kill you right away, but sure take away the fun for you and those who love you!

How about a part-time job doing something you love? My happy place in the summer between high school and college was working at a Christian Camp called Forest Home in the San Bernardino mountains. No one was unhappy there. Maybe you have kept a "summer camp job" in retirement in your back pocket, and it's time to explore whether that might be an option post-retirement.

You could also take a casual hobby to new levels now that you have the time to devote to it. I had a friend recently retire from military service and asked him how retirement was going. You know what he told me? He said, "R. J., I don't know what I like to do. I wish I had picked up a hobby years ago."

Or, you could return to school. Many public colleges and universities (and some private ones) offer free or reduced tuition to residents of a certain age, often starting at 60. Check a school's website for details or call the registrar's office. Most especially, there are thousands of young men and women who need encouragement and wisdom from someone like you.

How about volunteering in one of the hundreds of different programs that reach out to the economically and educationally challenged areas of your community? My mom would spend time reading to kids in the impoverished section of our town. It's one of my favorite memories of my mom from my growing-up years in Yakima, WA!

I have a friend, John, who is a retired attorney. Brilliant. He volunteers for a wonderful program here in San Diego called Reality Changers. He helps review the applications of those competing to enter college. These are kids who often are the first in their families to attend school past the 8th grade.

The opportunities to be blessed by being a blessing are all around us, and it will help to keep you young at the same time!

Action Items

1. What are you going to do once you're retired – make a list now and run it by your spouse/life partner and/or good friends. What are their reactions?
2. Schedule a "test run" as you get close to your target retirement date to see if what you think you want to do will be "fun" for the next 30 or more years!

The Purpose Behind the Pile

I have a confession. In the first draft of this book, the Five How Questions were originally the Four Hows. But as we worked through the frictions and the solutions to common retirement questions, we kept returning to "Why?"

Why is age 65 the accepted age for retirement, and what is retirement supposed to look like anyway?

Well, sometimes people spend their careers in arenas they do not like in order to put food on the table. That is a good reason to retire *from* something. But escape is different than a destination.

It brings to mind that scene from *Alice in Wonderland* by Lewis Carroll:

"Alice: Would you tell me, please, which way I ought to go from here?
The Cheshire Cat: That depends a good deal on where you want to get to.

Alice: I don't much care where.
The Cheshire Cat: Then it doesn't much matter which way you go.
Alice: ...So long as I get somewhere.
The Cheshire Cat: Oh, you're sure to do that, if only you walk long enough."

Perhaps my co-author and I have read too many goal-setting books. However, each and every one of them recommends having a strong "why" for every goal you set, no matter how big or small. Having a "why" gives you purpose behind the effort when things get hard … which they frequently do.

Since retirement is an awfully large goal, the Four How Questions morphed into the Five How Questions, with the addition of "How come?"

For some, that answer might be to get out of a job they hate. And, if that is you … we hope your "pile of wealth" gives you a springboard to something so great that you can't wait to leap out of bed in the morning. And, at the end of the day, you will have to be dragged to bed because you are so excited about how you are dedicating your time. (As my friend Max Bolka likes to say, "If you don't have something so exciting that you leap out of bed in the morning to get started, stay in bed until you figure something out!")

Whether you are continuing your purpose or entering a new phase of life in retirement, we remind you of the French approach to the word. The concept of retirement, as the French observed in the original meaning, is not about leaving the field of battle, never to return. Retirement is to step away for a time, maybe have a good meal and a great bottle of wine – or two – then return to action.

My experience over the decades is that as individuals develop their own personal answers to the first four of the Five How Questions, they build extraordinary confidence in themselves, their abilities, and in the future. As that confidence builds, it erupts into action like Old Faithful in Yellowstone National Park!

As you genuinely process "How much? How soon? How long? How many (buckets)?" you will gain the clarity you need to create your ideal retirement plan … and then take action toward achieving your goals.

So, how do we make it an *ideal* retirement?

In the last chapter, we included a link to Dr. Riley Moynes's TEDx talk on the Four Phases of Retirement.

To paraphrase his research, most people experience retirement in the following phases:

Stage 1: Vacation - I'm on vacation! What fun! Why didn't I do this sooner?

Stage 2: Depression - It's only been 12-18 months, and I am *so* bored. If these are supposed to be my "golden years," why do they feel like rust? Why do I feel so miserable and without purpose?

Stage 3: Trial & Error - OK, maybe it's time to get out of the rut and figure out what else I could do with my life.

Stage 4: Reinvent & Rewire - Oh my gosh, look out, world! This is what I was meant to do and to be!

We really are big fans of the Mark Twain quote, "The two most important days in your life are the day you are born and the day you find out why."

How many of those who, when they retire, are clear on the "why" they're here on the planet? We would submit for your consideration that perhaps the biggest reason why retirees go through depression is because they're not clear on their "why" purpose in life … and so they flounder.

Here's another radical thought for your consideration: Is it possible to skip directly from Stage 1 to Stage 3? It would seem that the best way to do that is by getting clear on "How come?" What difference has your life made thus far, or could it make, looking ahead, to impact your world in a lasting positive way?

One of my favorite authors and human beings, Dr. Ken Blanchard, captures this thought beautifully in the title of his co-authored book *Refire! Don't Retire: Make the Rest of Your Life the Best of Your Life.*

The "How come?" of retirement is an opportunity to create/refine your own meaning for your life … or change it if you don't like the answers you come up with.

No matter what age you are, whether you get paid for your purpose in U.S. dollars, social currency, or psychological satisfaction … your life matters! And you get to choose what that meaning is or will be. (Does this remind anyone of *It's A Wonderful Life*? It can be, you know!)

We are living in a very different world today than when the concept of retirement was invented … or even when *It's A Wonderful Life* was made.

In the old world, you worked until you died … or until you couldn't, and, hopefully, one of your children would take care of you.

In the new world, we're living longer. Most of us will reach "retirement age" now, and many will live decades beyond it.

There is an opportunity here for this to be the most impactful part of your life if you decide it will be that way. (We can't all be medical researchers curing cancer, but Mr. "11 herbs and spices" Colonel Sanders didn't begin franchising his secret recipe until age 62!)

So, please forgive me for being abrupt, but why are you here on the planet? Is there something that you always wanted to do that you told yourself you shouldn't/couldn't? What's holding you back from trying/doing/starting that in your retirement?

How about getting up early this coming Saturday with a legal pad and a cup of coffee and starting brainstorming?

- What do you love doing? What do you want to do more of?
- What do you hate doing, or at least want to do less of?
- What do you want to stop doing altogether?
- What do you want to start doing?
- When you look back over your life, what are the things, activities, places, and people that have brought you the greatest energy, delight, satisfaction, and encouragement?

And then, after all that good work, reward yourself with a margarita with a cute umbrella! (Non-alcoholic or high-octane. Your choice!)

How might your purpose from above fit in with your community, or what can you do so that someday your grandkids will be proud to say, "Grandma/pa did/built/created that!"

How amazing would THAT be …and feel?

Remember that saying, "You can't take it with you." It is true. Not that Egyptian pharaohs didn't *try* for centuries. Though we can't definitively say how that worked out in the afterlife, we do know that here on Earth, they sure made many grave robbers extremely wealthy!

OK, back to you (assuming you are not grave robbing). Building an enormous pile of wealth is a worthy goal that will hopefully keep you comfortable throughout your golden years.

But an *ideal* retirement? That's more than the dollar signs in all the buckets you can draw from for income. We suggest, for your consideration, that creating an *ideal* retirement (and we hope you feel the same) is having a purpose behind the pile. Something to:

- Do with your time
- Take responsibility for leaving a lasting positive impact
- Motivate you to get out of bed in the morning
- Leave a legacy that will make your children, grandchildren, friends, etc., very, very proud to have known you.

We hope that the tools we've shared throughout the book to build your ideal retirement will let you experience life to the fullest. And, as that becomes so, please don't keep it a secret. Please share what you learned. We hope that you are also able to assist those less fortunate than yourself.

How can we each show another today that they are precious and valued … just for who they are? Not for what they might provide or do for us or another … but simply because they are each made special by a loving and caring heavenly Father. They matter … and so do you!

Sharing these thoughts with you over the past few chapters has been an extraordinary privilege … one that we do not take lightly. You matter to us … and we are grateful to have been with you on the journey!

Our greatest hope is that it has been a blessing for you as well as you craft your ideal retirement.

P.P.S. If you have questions, suggestions, or need clarification, email or call us! info@wealthlegacygroup.com, and we do actually have a phone that, at least periodically, non-sales people call if you prefer that approach: (858) 569-0633.

SECTION 6

How to Start?

So ... If You Snoozed Off in One (or More) of the First 105 Pages, Humility Aside ... Here Are The Best Takeaways!

(My attorney, once again, reminds me to say that we are not *your* financial advisor and always to get specific advice from your financial professional.)

Step 1: Answer your Five How Questions

Build a plan based on the Five How Questions (think of it as Version 1; it will change later.) Break out your legal pad (or laptop) and begin crafting your answers to the Five How Questions:

1. **How come?** What are the reasons you want to retire someday? The more, the better!

2. **How much?** And is that annual income pre-tax or after-tax?
3. **How soon?** Be specific! To the month and the year! (And, a "how come then?" is a good question to answer, too!)
4. **How long?** (And, for simplicity, use age 100, although you can expect longer! Just sayin')
5. **How many (sources)?** So, IRAs, 401(k)s, Social (In)security, Insurance cash values, HSAs, rental real estate, etc. Make sure to have at least one that is non-taxable

Step 2: Identify an end amount and begin saving towards that within two weeks of today

- For many of us, it will mean setting aside an initially scary amount each month
- For most (depending upon your age now and your target age for retirement), it will mean roughly 17 - 20% of every paycheck needs to be sent ahead for your ideal retirement fund. Whoaaaa …
- Don't get discouraged! Even if you're only saving 2-3% of your paycheck right now, building a "positive addiction" to saving money is the goal of Step 2. (Read the book called *Tiny Habits!* It's brilliant!)
- Money loves speed. It's the action of beginning to save something and then increasing the percentage over time that will get you to your finish line. (And we'll be cheering you on!)

Step 3: Begin getting out of debt … starting today

- Make a list of everybody you owe money to and what interest rate you're paying them.
  - Credit card(s)
  - Home equity line of credit
  - Home mortgage
  - Student debt
  - Car loans
  - Etc.
- Focus your debt reduction payments on the debt paid off most quickly. Once you pay it off, put half of the money being spent towards the debt reduction into savings and the other half towards the debt next most quickly paid off.
- There are many great books on this topic. Check a couple out from your local library!

Step 4: Build your savings

- Begin filling your savings bucket with enough cash to eventually cover at least 3-6 months of expenses
  - 12-24 months if you're self-employed and/or own rental real estate
- Having money in savings will prevent you from adding *more* debt when surprise expenses occur … and they will … trust me!
- The rate of return is not as important as the accessibility of the money. If you need it for an emergency or opportunity, you need to have it available with no strings attached

Step 5: Implement "core" tax-advantaged and/or risk reduction strategies

- Health Savings Account … this is the #2 takeaway from this book. You need one … right now. Mark your calendar for open enrollment
- Cash-value-focused life insurance to grow assets without tax
- Interview and hire (when possible) a cross-disciplinary financial/planning advisor for their counsel and assistance
- Purchase the appropriate amounts of insurance to protect your hard work, aka your assets

Step 6: Max out contributions to your qualified retirement accounts

- But first, get your emergency fund in place!
- If money is tight, begin with contributing enough to your retirement program to at least maximize any employer match
    - In general, fund something towards your retirement to get your employer match, but not if it means nothing is going toward your emergency account
    - Find the balance between funding retirement vehicles, health care savings plans and having appropriate liquidity to cover emergencies
- Just because you can put more money in the retirement account doesn't mean you should

- Retirement accounts have a lot of IF/THEN decisions, refer to Section 4 - How Many? or your financial advisor for specifics

Step 7: Build a diversified portfolio of investments

- Next, once a solid financial foundation of investment real estate, equities, and fixed income is in place, consider adding other types of investments in small amounts - 5% or less - but don't venture off the path until it is well established
- Get comfortable with being very patient. Breaking free of earth's gravity, also known as "compound interest," takes time! Watching money work and grow is not exciting, at least in the early days, but it gets *really* exciting when it takes off! Be consistent! Tiny steps lead to giant "leaps" later on!

Step 8: Understand the role and vulnerability of Medicare and Social Security benefits

- Go online and create your Social Security system log-in and begin to understand its workings. Check out the old age, disability, and retirement benefit aspects of the system to understand how to maximize your benefits - https://www.ssa.gov/onlineservices/
- Medicare has never been more challenging to understand than now. We would encourage you to hire a specialist in this area by either paying a fee or purchasing insurance through them once you understand your options

- Compare your Social Security income stream beginning at age 62 vs. collecting your benefits at your "normal retirement age" (NRA) vs. delaying benefits as long as possible to allow it to compound (presently 8% compounding per year to age 70) and maximize the amount you receive
- Unless you are in poor health, it is normally best to defer beginning payments to age 70. Even with waiting 8 years, the much larger income stream makes deferring a better option, usually by age 81 or 82. Plus, by waiting to obtain the maximum benefit, your surviving spouse will receive the higher benefits should you predecease them

As a Registered Investment Advisor, I cannot guarantee anything, or my compliance attorney will put fish in my hubcaps. Nothing is guaranteed in life. But there is a very high probability that the sun will rise and the moon will set tomorrow. Likewise, if you follow the above recommendations and the further suggestions in the book, it is highly probable that you will find yourself celebrating a retirement beyond anything that you could have initially hoped for or imagined.

We are celebrating you and the remarkable journey you are on … and the lives you will touch for lasting good!

About R. J. Kelly

R. J. Kelly, AEP, CAP, ChFC, CLU, MSFS, RICP, WMCP, is known for his creativity, communication skills, and unique approach to planning.

He excels at quickly understanding complex, delicate situations and translating them into clear, actionable strategies. R. J. is a master at uncovering integrated, often-overlooked solutions through a holistic, multi-disciplinary lens.

He is the Founder and Chief Visionary Officer of Wealth Legacy Group®, Inc., based in San Diego, California. With clients in nineteen states and growing, WLG specializes in serving successful entrepreneurs, professionals, and their families with creative planning and legacy solutions.

www.ingramcontent.com/pod-product-compliance
Lightning Source LLC
LaVergne TN
LVHW052044200926
848481LV00005B/1729
* 9 7 8 1 9 5 4 7 5 7 7 0 7 *

www.ingramcontent.com/pod-product-compliance
Lightning Source LLC
LaVergne TN
LVHW022230200926
848481LV00006B/2210
* 9 7 9 8 2 9 5 4 5 0 2 8 0 *